Ex Líbrís

Jack Roland

Christmas '90 The Rosenbergs

CEDAR RAPIDS

Produced in cooperation with the
Cedar Rapids Area Chamber of Commerce

Windsor Publications, Inc.
Northridge, California

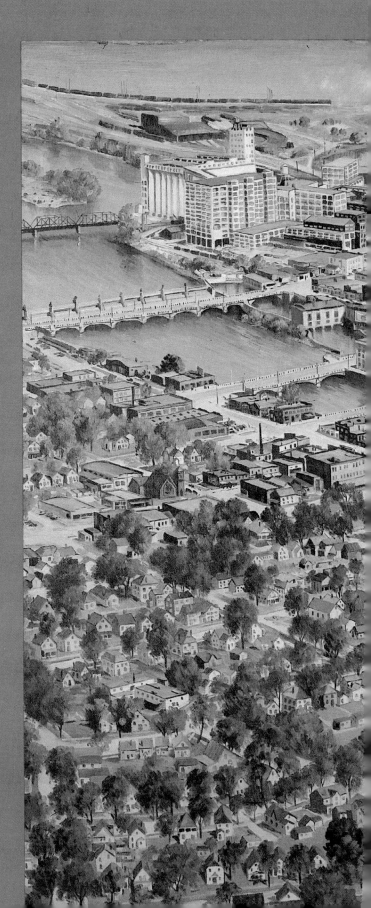

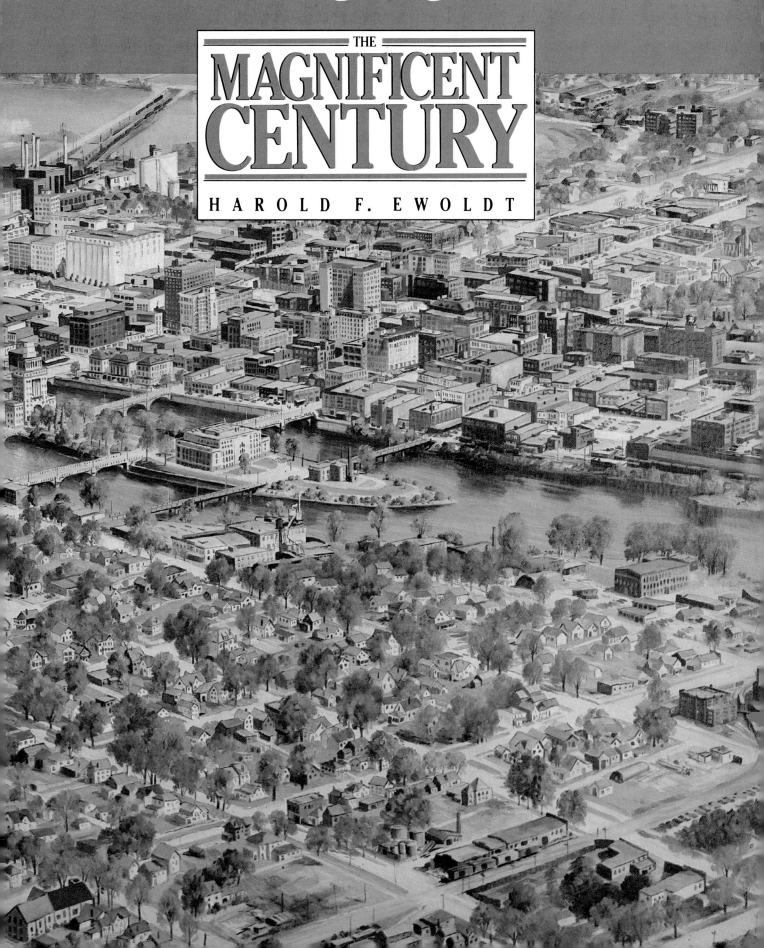

CEDAR RAPIDS

THE MAGNIFICENT CENTURY

HAROLD F. EWOLDT

This book is dedicated to my wife, Dorothy, and to my daughter, Susan,
both of whom have given me support and encouragement in my historical research
on Cedar Rapids and the Cedar Rapids area.

Windsor Publications, Inc.—History Books Division
Managing Editor: Karen Story
Design Director: Alexander D'Anca

Staff for *The Magnificent Century:*
Photo Director: Susan L. Wells
Associate Editor: Jeffrey Reeves
Manuscript Editor: Marilyn Horn
Production Editor, Business Biographies:
    Thelma Fleischer
Editor, Business Biographies: Judith L. Hunter
Senior Proofreader: Susan J. Muhler
Editorial Assistants: Didier Beauvoir, Alyson Gould, Kim
    Kievman, Michael Nugwynne, Kathy B. Peyser, Pat
    Pittman, Theresa Solis
Publisher's Representative: John Swedberg
Art Director: Christina L. Rosepapa
Layout Artist, Business Biographies: John T. Wolff
Layout Artist, Editorial: Michael Burg
Designer: Tanya Maiboroda

Library of Congress Cataloging-in-Publication Data
Ewoldt, Harold F.
    Cedar Rapids
    "Produced in cooperation with the Cedar Rapids
Area Chamber of Commerce."
    Bibliography: p. 131
    Includes index.
    1. Cedar Rapids (Iowa)—History. 2. Cedar Rapids
(Iowa)—Economic conditions. 3. Cedar Rapids (Iowa)—
Description—Views. 4. Cedar Rapids (Iowa)—Industries.
I. Cedar Rapids Area Chamber of Commerce. II. Title.
F629.C3E95   977.7'62   88-26177
ISBN: 0-89781-286-7

Windsor Publications, Inc.
Elliot Martin, Chairman of the Board
James L. Fish III, Chief Operating Officer

*Frontispiece: The modern city that Cedar Rapids has become is
a model of modern urban efficiency coupled with the beauty of
the countryside and serenity of the river. Courtesy, Iowa Electric
Light and Power Company*

CONTENTS

Osgood Shepherd, Cedar Rapids' first settler, built this tavern in 1838. Courtesy, Iowa Electric Light and Power Company

EDWIN J. BRUNS

PART 1

The LAND

Rural Cedar Rapids brings back memories of a society soley dependent on agriculture. Photo by Paul Foote

EARLY AGRICULTURE AND MARKETING

First there was the land.

To the early settlers, the Plains, of which Linn County is a very small part, must have seemed to be an endless sea of waving waist-high prairie grass, dotted with trees, bushes, and ponds. It stretched as far as the eye could see, a lush and fertile land that had limitless resources of water, wood, and wildlife.

Hunters and trappers had crisscrossed the area in the 1830s. In the summer of 1837 an opportunistic hunter and trapper, Osgood Shepherd, arrived in the Cedar Rapids area, liked it, and built a cabin on the east side of the river where First Street and First Avenue now come together. Shepherd was followed by several individuals and families who were interested in homesteading in 1838 and 1839, but it was not until 1840 that farmers came to Linn County.

In the year 1840 the United States experienced one of its periodic mass migrations of people moving west to the frontier. The lure was cheap government land. The government widely advertised the millions of acres of fertile land available in a mysterious region known as the Territory of Iowa. Motivated and inspired by this prospect, thousands of young farm families loaded their possessions into beat-up wagons pulled by a pair of stolid oxen and headed for this frontier of opportunity.

The first census of Linn County in 1840 reported 1,373 persons. By 1850 the population of the county had grown to 5,444. In the 1850s, Germans and Czechs—enticed by the promise of inexpensive land—cascaded into Linn County, and by 1860 the population had grown to 18,947.

This mass migration came from western New York, western Pennsylvania, and eastern Ohio. Some came overland, but most took turnpike roads and canals down to the Ohio River, booked passage on a river steamer, and sailed along the Ohio to St. Louis where they took a smaller boat to the river towns of Keokuk or Muscatine. From there they journeyed inland through a sea of prairie grass.

They traveled an average of 10 or 11 miles a day in good weather, camping along the way, until they reached a spot where no one had staked out a farm or put up a cabin. In 1840 and the 15 years that followed, Linn County was as far as they had to go. This was the frontier.

Before the influx of white settlers into the area, Indian tribes hunted, fished, and grew crops in Cedar Rapids. Painting by Edwin J. Bruns, Courtesy, Iowa Electric Light and Power Company

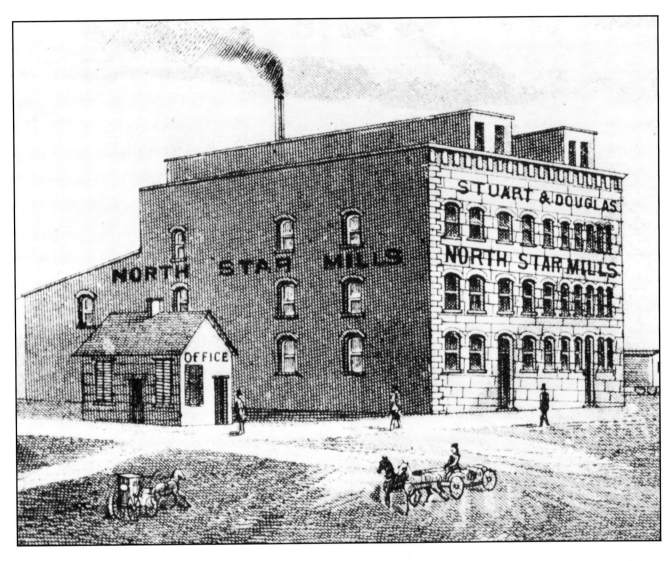

Above: This 1875 view of the North Star Mills, started in 1873 by Robert Stuart and George Douglas, Sr., is a very rare image. From Andreas, Historical Atlas of Iowa, *1875*

Opposite: This drawing of the Cedar Rapids railroad station depicts the terminal as it looked in the 1860s or 1870s. It stood at Fourth Street and First Avenue, and served the community until the Union Depot was built in 1896.

lage. Farmers could butcher hogs late in November to sell in town, but the quantity was governed by local demand. There were no other markets. Dressed hogs sold for only $1.50 per 100 pounds. It was an uncertain market for all concerned.

Hopes for an improved market for agricultural products surfaced in 1856 with news that a railroad was being laid from Clinton, on the Mississippi River, to Linn County. Slowly and painfully, track was laid for this railroad. Its construction pace ebbed and flowed with the sale of bonds that financed it at $18,000 per mile. Its construction was continually in doubt as the disposition of a state land grant shifted to the railroad that would run from Marion to Cedar Rapids and back. Eventually the land grant went to Cedar Rapids.

The railroads greatly increased land development in Cedar Rapids. Development was also aided by banking, which started in 1852. Using land warrants given to veterans of the War of 1812 and the Mexican War as units of commercial exchange, the banks did a lively business financing land purchases. Railroads, meanwhile, used the sale of government-granted land to encourage migration to the area.

By 1856 both Marion and Cedar Rapids carried listings of land offices and agencies in their city directories. These listings included such names as Whittam & Belt, Bates and Tousley, Carpenter Lehman and Company, and H. Mount and Company. Many of these land companies were controlled by John I. Blair, a railroad and land-development entrepreneur from New Jersey. At one time in his career Blair controlled 17 railroad companies, owned over two million acres of government land grants, and was principal stockholder in several banks.

On June 11, 1859, the Chicago, Iowa, and Nebraska Railroad arrived in Cedar Rapids amid the cheering of over 1,500 people from the town and surrounding area. This new mode of transportation would combine with river waterpower to create the industrial character of Cedar Rapids. It was now possible to get supplies in and ship products out quickly and efficiently.

With the arrival of the railroad, agriculture could now tap the cash market in Chicago. A new type of business—the commission house—was set up in both Cedar Rapids and Marion. These establishments purchased livestock from the farmers and shipped it to Chicago for a profit. The farmers, after assessing this new potential, shifted their production from wheat to corn. They could feed the corn to cattle and hogs, sell the livestock to the commission houses, and get a badly needed commercial commodity—cash. Hog production could now supply an important cash income to the farmers.

Those who continued to grow wheat could still sell it to the mills, but could also sell their surplus to the same commission houses, who shipped it to Chicago. It was a highly satisfactory arrangement for all concerned. Agriculture would now enter a new marketing era.

Top: This view of the Quaker Oats Plant was photographed from the west side of the Cedar River in 1987. Courtesy, Donald Karr, Jr.

Bottom: George Douglas, Jr. (seen here), his father, and Robert Stuart founded the North Star Milling Company, now known as Quaker Oats. Douglas also founded the Douglas Starch Works (later Penick & Ford). From Brewer and Wick, History of Linn County, 1911

CORN
AND CEREAL
MILLING

From the end of the Civil War until 1870, another mass migration headed west for the frontier. These people originated from Illinois, Indiana, and Kentucky. The frontier had moved west to the western part of Iowa, the Nebraska Territory, and the Dakota Territory.

This time the immigrants did not have to walk but could ride the train for part of their journey. Because of this, Cedar Rapids was in an advantageous position. It was the railhead, the end of the line. Track was being laid west through Tama, Marshalltown, and eventually to Council Bluffs, but until 1870 people heading west had to get off the train at Cedar Rapids.

Cedar Rapids was where these westward-bound people bought their horses, wagons, clothing, plows, farm implements and tools, and food supplies for the trek overland to the western part of the state. The banks of the Cedar River from B Avenue down to Seventh Avenue proliferated with factories, mills, and warehouses, all designed to take care of the needs of these people. All enjoyed fantastic business, including the flour mills, which sold thousands of barrels of flour.

This prosperity in the milling industry attracted similar businesses, and in 1873 it would bring Robert Stuart and George Douglas to Cedar Rapids. They and the business they started would take Cedar Rapids into a new economic era.

Robert Stuart and his father, John, were proprietors of the North Star Oatmeal Mill located near Ingersoll, Ontario, Canada. The market in that area was not big enough to absorb the capacity of their mill, and their production was limited to about 25 barrels a day. Seeking an exit from this dead-end commercial venture, the two Stuarts set out for the United States in 1873. Oatmeal was fast becoming a popular breakfast food, and they wanted to cash in on this new trend.

After carefully examining several regions of the country, they finally came to Iowa and settled in the Cedar Rapids area. This area had the best quality of oats in the country, and in abundant supply. The weather was ideal—cool enough in the spring to nurture the grain and hot enough in the summer to mature and dry it—and the location of Cedar Rapids for a mill was ideal, as attested by three waterpowered mills already in operation.

Above left: Nicholas S. Brown, a native of Connecticut, arrived in Cedar Rapids in 1842 while still a young man of 18. He erected the first mill, a gristmill, along the river, which began the city's milling industry. From Brewer and Wick, History of Linn County, *1911*

Above center: W.D. Watrous, operator of a flouring mill in the 1850s and 1860s, was active in several banks and insurance companies. He also served on the city council in 1856. From Andreas, Historical Atlas of Iowa, *1875*

Above right: George Douglas, Sr., patriarch of the Douglas family, was an early oatmeal manufacturer. This photograph was made circa 1880. From Laurance, Pioneer Days in Cedar Rapids, *1936*

Opposite, top: The Cedar Rapids Linseed Oil works was established in 1869 by R.D. Stephens and Sampson Bever. The business produced more than 200,000 gallons of linseed oil annually, plus 4 million pounds of oil cake and meal. This image was made in 1875. From Andreas, Historical Atlas of Iowa, *1875*

Opposite, bottom left: The Douglas Starch Works in 1914 was rated as the largest independent starch works in the world. Courtesy, Cedar Rapids Chamber of Commerce

Opposite, bottom right: This photograph reveals the destruction caused by the explosion at Penick & Ford (the former Douglas Starch Works) on May 22, 1919. Several days passed before rescue workers could sift through all the ruins for bodies. Courtesy, Donald Karr, Jr.

They purchased a site at D Avenue and Third Street, erected a three-story brick building that could be expanded, and then implemented a new idea for power. In partnership with Henry Higley, they bought a steam engine from a defunct woolen mill and began business. Their production was 300 barrels of oatmeal per day.

The Stuart-Higley partnership was dissolved in 1874, and the Stuarts entered into a partnership with George B. Douglas and his father, George Sr. That partnership would last until around the turn of the century.

North Star Oatmeal thrived in Cedar Rapids. Its production and storage facilities constantly increased. By 1888 the Cedar Rapids facility was known as the finest milling property in America. It rode the crest of a burgeoning industry, as oatmeal plants stretched from Nebraska to Ohio.

Shortly before the turn of the century, these 20-odd oatmeal plants consolidated into a conglomerate called Cereal Milling Company, which became the American Cereal Company. North Star Oatmeal was part of this conglomerate. The trade name "Quaker," and the figure of a man dressed in typical Quaker fashion became well-known all over the United States and Europe.

The entire Cedar Rapids complex, including four elevators filled with over one million bushels of oats, was razed to the ground by a fire on March 7, 1905. In less than 12 hours, one of the most disastrous and spectacular fires in the city's history devastated an industry that gave employment to 800 people.

Fortunately for the community, the decision was

made to rebuild the plant in Cedar Rapids. Its corporate name was changed to the Quaker Oats Company, and it was again in operation.

Since the fire of 1905, continual physical improvements and production innovations have been made. New brands of oatmeal, poultry and animal feeds, cornmeal, pancake flour, furfural, and many kinds of dry cereal have been added to the product line throughout the years.

George B. Douglas severed his connection with the North Star Oatmeal Company in 1891 when it became a part of the oatmeal conglomerate. However, he remained in touch with the grain-milling industry. In 1894 Douglas and his brother Walter organized the Douglas Company for the manufacture of linseed oil.

The linseed-oil industry had been established in Cedar Rapids in 1869 by R.D. Stephans and Sampson C. Bever who set up the Cedar Rapids Linseed Oil Company. Although it started out with a very limited production capacity, by 1875 the company was one of the leading industries of Central Iowa. It consumed about 100,000 bushels of flaxseed annually, from which was manufactured over 200,000 gallons of linseed oil, plus

four million pounds of linseed-oil cake and meal. The oil found its market in Eastern cities, while the cake and meal were exported to Europe.

The Douglas brothers operated their mill until 1899 when they sold it to the American Linseed Company, probably foreseeing that the industry was running its course. The enterprising Douglas brothers also had another industry in mind, one that would make a large imprint on the economy of Cedar Rapids.

In 1903 the brothers organized Douglas & Company for the manufacture of cornstarch. Douglas & Company soon developed into the largest starch industry west of the Mississippi River, processing 6,000 bushels of corn a day. The company also produced a myriad of other consumer goods including food products, beer, soap, and paper ingredients. By 1919 it was processing 20,000 bushels of corn daily.

On May 22, 1919, a massive explosion destroyed the entire plant in a blinding flash. The blast broke every window in the downtown area; chunks of concrete and bricks were hurled for miles. An immense amount of rubble and debris was all that remained of the large plant. Forty-three people lost their lives in the explosion. The cause of the disaster was never agreed upon. The chaos and clean-up work consumed weeks afterward.

For a few months following the explosion, much doubt existed as to whether the plant would be rebuilt. Most of the stockholders took back their investment money out of the insurance settlements until only the Douglas interest remained. George Douglas held the organization together until it could be offered to a new company that would rebuild the plant. In December 1919 the property was sold to Penick and Ford Ltd., Inc., then processing sugar-cane syrup and molasses at Harvey, Louisiana.

Top: The Penick & Ford Plant in 1921 was being rebuilt from the ruins of Douglas Starch Works after the disastrous 1919 explosion. Courtesy, Donald Karr, Jr.

Bottom: John C. Reid, founder of the National Oats Company, moved the business to Cedar Rapids in 1910 from East St. Louis. He served as president of the Chamber of Commerce in 1928-1929, and chaired an emergency food committee during the Depression years. Courtesy, Cedar Rapids Chamber of Commerce

Rebuilding the wrecked plant began in April 1920, and by February 1921 the plant was again operating. More than eight million dollars was invested in rebuilding costs during that year. From that time on, the company's products and volume were constantly increased. Under its new name, Penick and Ford, the business became a quiet but substantial part of the industrial community. It experienced steady growth, and by 1965 employed 1,000 people.

In that year the company began to go through a number of corporate and operating changes. Penick and Ford was acquired by the R.J. Reynolds Tobacco Company, and was operated as a wholly owned subsidiary. It was not a very happy or very long union. Reynolds became involved in an antitrust lawsuit with the Justice Department as a result of the acquisition. Operating and labor problems continued to mount, and in 1968 plant employees went on strike for three months.

Reynolds finally settled its dispute with the Justice Department, and in 1971 sold the plant to VWR United Corporation of Seattle. In 1977 VWR United Corporation made the reluctant decision to mothball the plant while it reassessed an overcapacity in the industry and sharply reduced sugar prices.

Starting in 1980 the corn-processing facility went through some major remodeling, and was restructured into a separate division of the parent company. By November 1981, four-and-a-half years after its mothballing, Penick and Ford went back into the full-time corn-milling business. In 1984 it was spun off into a separate

This photograph of the National Oats Plant was made circa 1914, when John Reid moved here from East St. Louis to take charge of operations. Note the fire bell in the background. Courtesy, Donald Karr, Jr.

corporate structure under which it is now operating.

Another early member of the Cedar Rapids corn- and grain-milling community got its start in East St. Louis, Illinois, in 1904. Two young men, J.G. Matthews and John C. Reid, scraped together an investment of $10,000 in wagons and tools and $25,000 in machinery, hired 14 employees, and started the Corno Mills Company.

Their product was Corno Feeds, an animal feed for horses and mules. This feed contained just four ingredients—corn, hominy feed, alfalfa, and oat feed. To meet their constantly increasing need for oat feed, a byproduct of rolled oats, Reid and Matthews decided to get into the rolled-oats business. They purchased the Stobie Cereal Mills in Peoria, and later the Pawnee Mills in Cedar Rapids. With these purchases, they changed their corporate name to National Oats Company to reflect the diversity of the business.

Upon the purchase of Pawnee Mills in 1910, Reid and his family moved to Cedar Rapids. During World War I the Cedar Rapids plant operated at full capacity to supply rolled oats to the United States and the Allies. At the end of the war, all the cereal operations of National Oats were concentrated in Cedar Rapids.

In 1922 a new process was discovered for making rolled oats that cooked much more quickly. Rather than 20 to 30 minutes, the new product took only three minutes to prepare. "Three-Minute Oats" became an instant success and completely altered the emphasis for National Oats. In 1924 the company began to shift the entire management structure to Cedar Rapids.

In the late 1940s National Oats' product line became even more successful. Television was becoming very popular in American homes, and the company decided to enter the popcorn field, recognizing that popcorn would be a great accompaniment to television viewing. Again, National Oats had a new product that gained instant success. The company's popcorn business almost overshadowed its oatmeal business. The new enterprise served national and international markets, and National Oats' Wall Lake plant, serving as the principal processing and storage facility, became the largest popcorn plant in the world.

By 1967 the needs of capital structure began to emerge. National Oats Company was sold to Liggett & Myers Tobacco Company and operated as a wholly owned subsidiary. In January 1980 Liggett sold the company to a combine of Curtice-Burns, Inc., and Pro-Fac Cooperative, Inc., of Rochester, New York. Under this new structure, National Oats has continued its steady market influence and production, maintaining a consistent employment of around 300.

Cargill, Inc., headquartered in Minneapolis, entered the milling community of Cedar Rapids very quietly. It had opened a grain marketing office in the city in the 1930s. In 1945 its feed division, Nutrena, started manufacturing animal nutrition products. Also during the 1940s, it operated the Iowa Milling Company, a soybean-processing operation.

In May 1967 a lease arrangement with Joseph Sinaiko provided Cargill with its first corn-milling operation in the Cedar Rapids area. Cargill acquired the corn-processing facilities of Corn Starch and Syrup Company plus other Sinaiko interests in Cedar Rapids. The corn plant, located at 1710 Sixteenth Street S.E., had the capacity to process 14,000 bushels of corn per day into starch, syrup, and gluten feed products. This arrangement gave Cargill processing facilities for soybeans and animal feeds.

In 1970 a corporate decision was made to devote the facility at 1120 Twelfth Street S.W. entirely to soybeans, which were then emerging as a world-wide commodity. This proved to be a wise decision, and in 1983 the Twelfth Street plant was expanded to improve the soybean specialties area and new-product development. This quiet enhancement of operation and product development continues to be characteristic of Cargill.

In marked contrast to Cargill, the entrance of General Mills into Cedar Rapids was heralded with fanfare and publicity. In January 1969 General Mills announced that it would construct a food-processing plant on Cedar Rapids' far southwest side which officials predicted would become the firm's largest facility in Iowa. This new plant would manufacture innovative new products for America's dinner table.

Construction started on May 6, 1969, at a 70-acre tract on Edgewood Road. Ground breaking and an excavation explosion was witnessed by a gathering of community officials. By mid-1970 the plant was producing high-protein soybean-based foods flavored with beef, poultry, and ham.

This first plant was not even finished when a second plant was started in February 1970. The second plant was designed to turn out convenience foods for restaurants, hospitals, schools, and vending machines. Although highly automated, these two plants, when put into operation, employed over 200 people. In 1978 General Mills expanded the two plants and switched production to ready-to-eat dry cereals, a move that resulted in job expansion.

By 1981 the plant complex had been enlarged to 300,000 square feet, and it employed 330 people. The following year, additional cereal product lines resulted in additional hiring. Since then the record of General Mills has been consistent employment, production, and expansion.

The newest arrival in Cedar Rapids' grain-milling industry was announced on April 1, 1970. A short announcement was made approving the zoning of land for industrial use at Waconia Avenue and Harnischfeger Drive S.W. The area was to be used for a wet corn-processing factory.

Ground breaking for this new corn-milling industry, named Corn Sweeteners, Inc., was held on May 28, 1970. Plans called for a fully automated corn-syrup plant, entirely self-contained, completely windowless, and built in a modular fashion that would permit incremental expansion. It was to be the most modern, efficient, and automated plant in the wet-milling industry. Costing in excess of five million dollars, the plant would cover 60,000 square feet, use about 10,000 bushels of corn daily, and would be capable of producing 1,400 tank cars of corn syrup per year. Employment was projected at about 100 people.

The Cargill Corn Processing Plant, one of three plants in Cedar Rapids operated by Cargill, was acquired from the Corn Starch and Syrup Company in 1967. The plant is located at 1710 16th St. S.E. Courtesy, Cedar Rapids Chamber of Commerce

Corn Sweeteners was destined for constant, positive change—in both operation and production. In April 1971, three months before the plant was ready for operation, Archer-Daniels-Midland Company announced that it would purchase a 50 percent interest in the company. This added capital permitted Corn Sweeteners to increase its production capability to approximately 75,000 bushels of corn per day. In April 1972 plans were announced to construct a new dextrose plant at the site. This meant increased employment.

By 1974 the possibility of fructose corn syrup for sweetening purposes was becoming an exciting reality. Another addition to the plant for the processing of high-fructose corn syrup was implemented. When the new facilities were completed in mid-1976, Corn Sweeteners was using 165,000 bushels of corn daily with 160 railcars in and out of the plant each day. The work force was at 250—a level that has been maintained consistently. It was the largest corn wet-milling plant in the world.

By 1977 there was intense speculation in the possibility of fructose corn syrup being used as a sweetening substitute by soft-drink manufacturers. Corn Sweeteners put another four million dollars in building

and equipment for the production of second- and third-generation fructose corn syrup. May 10, 1978, saw the successful start-up of the company's fructose corn-syrup production. On June 30 of that year, three major soft-drink manufacturers—Coca-Cola Co., Royal Crown Cola, and 7-Up—authorized their bottlers to increase the levels of fructose in their product.

With the fructose market safely tucked away, Corn Sweeteners turned its attention to producing alcohol for use in gasoline. In January 1980 plans were announced for an alcohol plant in Cedar Rapids. On July 7, 1981, this new plant was in full operation, consuming 50,000 bushels of corn and producing 125,000 gallons of water-free ethyl alcohol per day.

In 10 years, Corn Sweeteners had gone from a short announcement to the largest corn wet-milling plant in the world, a fitting close to a century of growth and progress in grain and cereal milling in Cedar Rapids.

Above left: Arthur T. Averill arrived in Cedar Rapids in 1865 and four years later organized Averill & Hamilton, an early farm implement firm. The business eventually became known as Hamilton Company. From Brewer and Wick, History of Linn County, *1911*

Top right: The Marion gang plow was manufactured by Marion Manufacturing Company. This particular piece of farm equipment was noted for its lightness of draft and maneuverability. It was a big improvement over the walking plow. From Andreas, Historical Atlas of Iowa, *1875*

Bottom right: Hamilton Seed and Coal Company, seen here in a 1930 photograph, was located on Rockford Road N.E. Courtesy, Cedar Rapids Chamber of Commerce

CHAPTER THREE

FEED, SEED,
AND
MACHINERY

Once a farmer had arrived in Linn County in the 1840s, constructed his first crude cabin, and established his claim, he found that he had several other needs to meet—adequate farm machinery, markets for his surplus, and increased and improved livestock production. It would take about a hundred years to overcome all of these challenges.

The basic tools a farmer brought with him were hoes, scythes, cradles, axes, and a simple cast-iron plow. It was soon found that this plow would not till the rich black dirt of the Iowa prairie. It took the combined efforts of the farmer, his wife and children, and a brace of stolid oxen to turn the virgin sod. Wheat and oats were seeded by hand; to plant corn, a farmer used a hoe and dropped the kernels into the hole. Using these methods, it was very difficult for a new farmer to get the required 10 acres under tillage the first year.

By 1847, however, steel plows became available. They were the principal product of a new factory established by John Deere & Company in Moline, Illinois. The Linn County farmers gladly made the difficult trip to Moline to bring back this prized piece of farm equipment. They also adapted quickly to the hand corn planter: a wedge-shaped point that, when jabbed into the ground, released several kernels of corn in the hole.

Technology in farm machinery developed rapidly. Soon manufacturers like Deere were turning out walking and riding cultivators, harrows, planters, mowers, rakes, grain seeders, and reapers, all designed to be horse-drawn.

This new technology was adopted by manufacturing entrepreneurs in Cedar Rapids. Farm machinery factories and warehouses sprang up along the riverfront, all the way from B Avenue to Seventh Avenue. These included the Star Wagon Works at Seventh Avenue and First Street, which turned out 1,200 to 1,500 wagons per year; the Tibbitts and Piper Carriage Works, which made about 900 wagons per year; the Williams Harvestor Company, which produced thousands of reapers and mowers; the Farmers Manufacturing Company, maker of sulky plows, harrows, rakes, stalkcutters, and cultivators; and the Grain Growers Manufacturing Company, which put out a line of stalkcutters, grain seeders, hayrakes, and later on, windmills.

Above: An early picture (circa 1870) of John T. Hamilton, who came to Cedar Rapids in 1869 to become a partner in Averill & Hamilton. The Hamilton family later acquired the Averill interest in the firm. Hamilton became interested in several banks, including Merchants National Bank. From Brewer and Wick, History of Linn County, *1911*

Opposite left: John G. Cherry, the founder of Cherry Burrell, was born in England and migrated to this area in 1869. After operating a general store at Troy Mills, he became a buttermaker at Walker, then moved to Cedar Rapids where he perfected a new type of cream can and began its manufacture. This photograph was taken circa 1880. Courtesy, Cherry Burrell

Opposite center: Walter L. Cherry was the oldest son of John G. Cherry. Upon the death of his father in 1899, Walter Cherry took over his father's food container business. His brothers, Howard H. and Herbert, later joined the firm. Walter was president of the Chamber of Commerce in 1918-1919. He died in 1946. Photo by Underwood, Washington. Courtesy, Cedar Rapids Chamber of Commerce

Opposite right: Howard H. Cherry, the youngest son of John G. Cherry, in his turn was president of Cherry Burrell, and served as president of the Chamber of Commerce in 1926. In 1927, he and a small group of business leaders raised funds for a new Chamber building. Courtesy, Howard Cherry, Jr.

Most of these manufacturers served a multi-county area and stayed in business until the late 1800s, when competition from firms such as McCormick, John Deere, J.I. Case, and Oliver would phase them out. For as long as they lasted, however, these local manufacturers made a substantial contribution to the industrial image of Cedar Rapids.

At first this new machinery had to be picked up by the farmer at the manufacturing plant. We do not find evidence of farm-implement dealers or distributors until around the Civil War, when advanced agricultural techniques were promoted by the newly created Department of Agriculture.

The Cedar Rapids business directory for 1869 listed six agricultural businesses. One of these early businesses, now known as the Hamilton Company, is still on the scene today. Arthur Averill arrived in Cedar Rapids in March 1865. In 1869 he induced his friend in Genesceo, Illinois, John T. Hamilton, to come to Cedar Rapids as his business associate. They organized the firm of Averill & Hamilton to deal in agricultural implements, seeds, coal, and kindred interests. The enterprise prospered from the beginning.

Eventually Averill disposed of his interests in the firm to John R. Amidon. In 1893 Hamilton's brothers, W.W. and Porter, acquired the Amidon holdings. The firm then operated as Hamilton Brothers. It became the most widely known implement house in the West, developing an extensive wholesale distribution in addition to its retail business. The Hamilton interests were eventually purchased by the Klinger family, and in recent years the business has been operated by the Chadima family.

After World War I, tractors and tractor-drawn machinery became more important in agriculture. Joseph M. Denning was one of the first in Cedar Rapids to try his hand at tractor manufacturing. The Denning Wire and Fence Company, established in 1899 to produce woven wire, was centered at 40 Eighth Avenue S.W. In the 1920s Denning had to bow to competition from the big tractor companies.

Despite the disappearance of Denning's firm, the mechanization of agriculture encouraged the establishment of large farm-machinery agencies in Cedar Rapids. These included Marak-Steffer Implement Company and Happel & Sons, both founded during the 1930s. The 1940s saw another spurt in the farm-machinery industry. The United States recognized it would have to feed all of its Allies during World War II, and most of the world after the war. The federal gov-

ernment encouraged increased technology in agriculture to produce this badly needed food. Farm machinery dealers such as Schwitters, Inc., set up operations at this time.

A decline in world consumption of our agricultural products in the 1980s has posed new challenges to farm-machinery manufacturers and agricultural-implement dealers.

Improvement of farm machinery in the 1870s aided the farmer in the Cedar Rapids area in greatly improving his agricultural production. But it left him with the problem of what to do with the surplus milk from his increasing herd of cows. The milk could be made into butter, but the town market for this home-made butter was limited.

In 1872 the first commercial creamery set up near Manchester. It was an instant success, and creameries sprang up all over the state. The cheese and butter produced at these creameries was in high demand in the East.

One of the area's important creameries was the Walker Creamery, built in 1877-1878. This creamery employed a young butter maker by the name of John G. Cherry. While at Walker, Cherry invented an ingenious milk-can top. The false bottom of this top extended into the can to the level of the milk, preventing it from churning while being transported. Cherry also conceived the idea of manufacturing a jacketed cream can which would be cool in the summer and prevent freezing in the winter. He secured patents on these inventions and in 1880 set up a small backyard workshop at his home in Cedar Rapids. This was the start of the J.G. Cherry Company. In time the company manufactured egg-case fillers,

butter machinery, ice-cream equipment, and an array of dairy machinery.

From this humble beginning and the eventual merger with seven allied industries has emerged the Cherry Burrell Corporation, the country's largest exclusive manufacturer of equipment for the handling of milk and milk products. A part of AMCA International Corporation since 1975, Cherry Burrell continues to improve its products and to expand its national and international markets.

Coinciding with the rise of the dairy-equipment industry was the creation of a new type of business: the feed supplement industry. This industry was spurred by the increase in livestock production that was encouraged by the federal government during World War I.

The first in the Cedar Rapids area to take advantage of this new business was a veterinarian in Stanwood, Dr. E.B. Fenton. In 1912 he started using "Mineratone" to treat necro, flu, and colitis in hogs. He also introduced a feed that took the place of protein substance at a lower cost and a higher gain. After 1924 this feed supplement was known as Vigortone, and its use would be broadened to cattle, poultry, and horses.

In 1922 Fenton moved his operation to Cedar Rapids. Through a unique network of neighborhood salespeople, Fenton expanded his sales network from southeastern Iowa to the entire state. Harness racehorses, as well as many saddle and running horses became users of the feed supplement. Orders began coming in from throughout the United States and Canada.

By 1938 the company was doing in excess of two

Top: Approximately 1,500 people were employed at the old Cherry Burrell plant on Tenth Avenue S.E., which became obsolete after World War II. Its operations were shifted into the present plant on Sixth Street S.W. in 1948. Photo by Thompson Photographers. Courtesy, Cedar Rapids Chamber of Commerce

Bottom: This rarely seen circa 1880 drawing depicts the first factory operated by John G. Cherry. At first turning out only cream cans, it eventually produced egg cases, egg case fillers, and related articles. Courtesy, Cherry Burrell

million dollars of business a year, shipping out several carloads of the feed to its customers every day. Known later as the Vigortone Company, it introduced new products each year. Under the managerial direction of the Fenton and Swartzendruber families, the Vigortone Company continued to expand its production and its sales.

In 1966 the company was acquired by Beatrice Foods, who guided its operations to new heights and into a new plant on Council Street N.E. in 1976. In 1984 Beatrice sold the operation to Pacific Molasses. The firm continues to be a viable force in the feed industry.

In 1922, as the Vigortone Company was being started in Cedar Rapids, R.P. Andreas was laying the foundation for another giant feed business in the area. A retired farmer, Andreas took over the R.J. Fiala grain, coal, and seed business in Lisbon. The Lisbon elevator was part of the deal. Andreas started manufacturing mixed feeds at Lisbon in 1927 on a small scale, with only a local sales territory.

In 1930 the company installed molasses tanks and a feed mixer. This introduction of corn molasses to the feed trade triggered spectacular growth for the company, expanding its sales territory to all of Iowa,

Illinois, and other Midwestern states. By the end of 1934, Andreas' Honeymead Products occupied a place of eminence in the feed world. By this time Andreas' four sons were in the business.

In 1936 Honeymead transferred its manufacturing base to Cedar Rapids, taking over the facilities of the Mesquakie Mills at 1120 Twelfth Avenue S.W. There it pioneered pellet feeds, an innovation that revolutionized the feed industry. This facility was eventually leased to the Nutrena Division of Cargill, as the Andreas family shifted its business interests elsewhere. The Honeymead facility became the west-side soybean plant of Cargill.

The Iowa Milling Company entered the livestock-feed business in Cedar Rapids in 1923. It manufactured a feed known as Vitamo which included a complete line of poultry feed, plus high protein feed supplements for cattle and hogs. Iowa Milling's soybean-processing operation brought it to the attention of Cargill, who eventually purchased the company.

The latest arrival in the Cedar Rapids feed industry came in 1943 when C.W. Bloomhall, a retired Penick and Ford executive, formed Diamond V Mills to manufacture a dry cultured yeast feed supplement. Located first at 132 E Avenue N.W., the operation moved in 1947 to a two-story plant that had been formerly occupied by the Otto Manufacturing Company. The rapid success of the product again required larger quarters, and in 1953 the facilities of Superlife Yeast Company were acquired.

Under the innovative direction of the Bloomhall family, Diamond V Mills has acquired a national and an international market. International sales account for nearly 10 percent of its volume.

In November 1985 the company shifted production to 436 G Avenue N.W. This new plant uses the very latest in automation, and production has doubled. With its market expansion and its new plant facilities, Diamond V Mills is the nation's largest manufacturer of cultured yeast.

In the Cedar Rapids of the late 1980s, the farm-machinery factories along the river have disappeared, phased out by the giant machinery manufacturers. These giants, in turn, are experiencing problems because of changing economic trends. These changes, however, have not affected the city's dairy-equipment businesses, nor is there any recession in the feed-supplement business. Both are in good shape and continue to contribute to the economy of the Cedar Rapids area.

Below left: The 1983 plant of Diamond V Mills, located at 200 E. Avenue N.W. (formerly occupied by Superlife Yeast) proved inadequate, and enlarged facilities were acquired. The company is still in constant expansion. Courtesy, Diamond V Mills

Below right: C.W. Bloomhall founded Diamond V Mills in 1943. Bloomhall was a retired Penick & Ford executive whose formula for manufacturing a dry-cultured yeast feed supplement met with instant success. The third generation of the Bloomhall family is now in the firm's management structure. Courtesy, Diamond V Mills

Top left: The Cedar Rapids Paper Box Factory (seen here in the 1860s or 1870s) was located along the Cedar River, like many other Cedar Rapids manufactories. Interestingly, this drawing shows women working at production jobs. From Andreas, Historical Atlas of Iowa, *1875*

Top right: This is an 1875 illustration of the Cedar Rapids Planing Mill Company, one of several sash and door factories operating during this period. From Andreas, Historical Atlas of Iowa, *1875*

Bottom: The Sinclair Packing Plant was photographed in the 1920s by William Baldridge. Courtesy, Cedar Rapids Chamber of Commerce

ENTERPRISE
ON THE
WATERFRONT

I n the early days of the community, the riverfront was lined not only with flour and grain mills, but also with machine shops, lumber mills, and several other businesses, all spawned by the river and its cheap, inexhaustible water power. At the start, these river enterprises were propelled by water power; later, water power was supplemented and eventually supplanted by steam power.

In 1850 George Greene founded the city's first furniture factory with the firm of Greene, Legare and Company. This chair and bedstead factory was completely propelled by water. In 1856 this enterprise was joined by a planing mill operated by Alexander Hagen, a lumber mill operated by Greene and Graves, and a sawmill and chair factory put up by Dobbs & Dewey. The Dobbs & Dewey factory had a capacity of about 10,000 feet of lumber a week, and during a year could turn out about 8,000 chairs, 1,000 bedsteads, and other miscellaneous articles of furniture. It employed 12 men.

The Greene and Graves mill had a capacity of processing about 5,000 feet of lumber daily. It also had a machine shop attached to it. The mill started out being powered by water, but by the late 1850s had converted to steam to keep pace with its expanding business. By 1858 it employed 25 men and manufactured all kinds of wood and iron machinery, including an early type of plow. The superintendent of this factory was Stephan L. Dows, who went on to make his name in the community.

In 1861 G.B. St. John also established a business along the river. His foundry and machine shop was soon elevated to one of the leading manufactories of Central Iowa, constructing and repairing all types of engines and machines.

A new type of river industry made its appearance in 1863 when Isaac Shaver arrived to set up a cracker factory at First Street and Fourth Avenue. The first cracker factory west of the Mississippi River used "Iowa Oyster" as its trademark. This business became the Shaver and Dows Cracker Factory in 1866 when Stephan Dows joined the firm. The factory's own cooperage turned out the barrels and boxes it needed for production and shipping. Its sales territory covered not only all of Iowa, but also surrounding states. Shaver and Davis was one of the leading industries of the city, employing about 70 men. The cracker plant was purchased by the New

Above left: William Greene, the younger brother of Judge George Greene, was involved in many business ventures with his brother, including a general store and the BCR&N Railway (in 1868). From Brewer and Wick, History of Linn County, *1911*

Above right: Isaac H. Shaver founded Shaver & Dows Cracker Factory in 1863. It was the first cracker factory west of the Mississippi River. From Laurance, Pioneer Days in Cedar Rapids, *1936*

Opposite left: This illustration of the retail store of H.G. Angle dates from around 1860. The store retailed dry goods, groceries, and glassware. Angle also operated a flour mill along the river. This building was also an early home of the Crescent Lodge. From Morcombe, History of Crescent Lodge, *1906*

Opposite right: The ice truck fleet of Hubbard Ice as it appeared in 1930. At that time, almost every home had an ice box. Courtesy, Cedar Rapids Chamber of Commerce

York Biscuit Company in 1890, but, soon after its purchase, the expensive operation was closed down.

The year 1876 saw a small woodworking mill start operations to serve the building needs of the growing city. Initially using the available water power, the mill later shifted to the west side of the river and steam power. This was the Williams and Hunting Company, long one of the leading millworking operations in the city, and one that existed up to very modern times.

In spite of all of this activity along the riverfront, the local newspaper of the time, the *Cedar Valley Times*, continued to blast away at local financiers and entrepreneurs for not exploiting the manufacturing capability of the city. The paper pointed out the power potential of the river and that it was not being tapped to its full capacity. It trumpeted the great need for a fanning mill factory, a stove factory, a papermill, and a pail and tub factory.

The newspaper editorials did their job, as these types of factories showed up in the industrial directories of subsequent years. Also making their appearance in due time would be factories turning out buggies, harnesses, saddles, and all types of equipment needed for the horse and carriage trade.

The newspaper editors of the day must have been well pleased in 1878 when J.H.B. and W.A. Otto established the North Star Shirt factory, a considerable industrial addition to the economy of the city. This factory, located along First Street, employed 25 people in 1881. The name of the firm would have indicated that only shirts were made, but such was not the case. Each month thousands of yards of cotton cloth were made into pants and overalls. North Star's products had an excellent reputation throughout the state. An interesting part of the operation was the extensive laundry connected to the factory.

By 1880, the start of our Magnificent Century, the city boasted 75 manufacturers, mostly extended along First Street and the river, from D Avenue down to Seventh Avenue. These riverfront industries and businesses produced seven million dollars in goods annually, and had a payroll well in excess of one million dollars a year.

During the spring, summer, and fall, the Cedar River produced the power that made possible the ever-expanding industries along its banks. During the winter and early spring, the river made possible another industry of the city: ice harvesting.

The ice industry was for the strong and the hardy. Back-bending work was required in the worst of climatic conditions to harvest this crop of the river.

Ice as a business venture in Cedar Rapids had its start in 1870 when Charles P. Hubbard and a "Commodore" Myers founded what was to become the Hubbard Ice Company. The business was started on the east side just above the dam site, but shifted to the west side in the 1880s. The firm of Hooper and Hubbard lasted until 1882, when Hubbard became sole owner. In 1902 it was incorporated as the Hubbard Ice Company.

By 1910 it had become one of the leading industries of the city, annually putting out 30,000 tons of ice. At its beginning, its capacity was only 1,500 tons. In 1915 the business was modernized by the addition of equipment to artificially manufacture ice.

Joseph T. Chadima was born in Cedar Rapids in 1870, the same year Charles Hubbard was starting his ice business. In 1900 Chadima embarked on his own business career as a dealer in ice and coal. His brother Thomas joined him in the business, which became the Chadima Brothers Ice and Coal Company. By 1911 they were putting out 15,000 tons of ice.

In 1922 Chadima Brothers merged with Hubbard Ice and Coal. In 1930 the company dropped the coal business and adopted the new method of heating with fuel oil. It also changed its name that year to Hubbard Ice and Fuel Company. Another step forward was made in 1940 by the addition of cold storage facilities. The enterprise is still operated by the Chadima family.

Another waterfront enterprise in Cedar Rapids began with the dream of an Irishman. In 1871 a young man stood on the banks of the Cedar River, studying the swirling waters. Unlike Nicholas Brown and Alexander Ely, he didn't visualize a sawmill, a gristmill, or a flour mill. Instead he visualized a pork-packing plant.

Thomas M. Sinclair carried with him the optimism of youth—he was barely 29—and the background of a pork-packing family in Ireland. The J & T Sinclair Company, meat provisioners, had been established in 1832 in Belfast. In addition to the packing business, the firm operated the largest and finest fleet of sailing vessels in Ireland.

After setting up a branch in Liverpool, the firm decided to establish a branch in the United States.

Above: Thomas M. Sinclair selected Cedar Rapids as the site for a pork-packing plant in 1871. The city was the center of a pork producing area and was located on a river that provided an adequate water supply. Sinclair died in 1881 as a result of a fall at the plant. Courtesy, Cedar Rapids Chamber of Commerce

Above right: T.M. Sinclair rented this vacant ice house at Fifth Avenue and First Street S.E. in 1871 for the first operations of his pork-packing plant. It was used for several seasons. Courtesy, Cedar Rapids Chamber of Commerce

Opposite top: This view from the river captures the Sinclair Packing Company at around the turn of the century. From Brewer and Wick, History of Linn County, *1911*

Opposite bottom: Shown here is the Wilson & Company packing plant as it appeared in 1971, the 100th anniversary of the company. The firm acquired the name Wilson & Company in 1935. Photo by Vern Thompson. Courtesy, Cedar Rapids Chamber of Commerce

Thomas Sinclair and his cousin, John Sinclair, were sent to New York City in 1862 to open a pork-packing plant there. The plant they built cured hams and bacon for export to Europe, and was open for about 12 years.

In August 1871 Thomas Sinclair decided to see what industrial advantages the Western part of the country might hold. He traveled to Duluth, Minneapolis and St. Paul, Winona, Dubuque, and then to Cedar Rapids. Impressed with the possibilities of Cedar Rapids, Sinclair decided to start a packing house in the city and to export pork to England.

Sinclair rented an ice house on the riverbank between Fourth and Fifth avenues. A makeshift operation at best, this facility was used only for the winter of 1871-1872. It had a space for lard rendering, a space for slaughtering, a space for the chilling of dressed hogs, and a space for the cutting of carcasses. The rest of the building was used for curing. Sinclair had picked a practical location for his start. It served to get the business going, and the river carried the residue away.

The following year another site was secured along the riverfront. This new location was further to the south and beyond the city limits (there had been local objection to a pork-packing plant within the city). Buildings were erected, and for seven years the plant made steady progress. In 1878 it processed 338,941 hogs. A year later the plant had a major fire and the slaughterhouse was destroyed. Fire continued to plague the operation, but after each fire better buildings were built and more modern machinery installed.

Sinclair died in 1881 in a tragic accident at the plant. The management was successively held by various members of the Sinclair family after his death. In 1906 a new plant was constructed at the same site.

Much of this structure existed until recent years.

The bulk of the plant's product was exported to England. When the pork-export market began to decrease in 1910, the Sinclair Company attempted to substitute domestic trade but without much success. In August 1913 financial problems forced the company to sell out to Sultzberger and Sons, but it continued to operate under the Sinclair name.

In 1916 Sultzberger had financial problems and was restructured under the presidency of a young man, Thomas E. Wilson. After the restructuring, the parent firm's name was changed to Wilson & Co., one of the "big four" in the meat industry by 1935. Wilson & Co. supplied fresh and processed meat products to markets principally in the Midwest and Northeast, as well as to foreign markets.

The 1940s saw the firm become the largest employer in Cedar Rapids with more than 2,500 on the payroll. During the 1960s and 1970s, there was a succession of corporate structural changes in the company. In December 1968 it became a wholly owned subsidiary of Ling-Temco-Vought, a Dallas-based aerospace and electronics concern. The local plant operated under the name Wilson-Sinclair, then Wilson

Foods, under a company-wide reorganization.

Since 1984 the plant, acquired by Keith Barnes, has operated under the name of Farmstead Foods, Inc. Employment has stabilized and plans are under way for renovation and growth.

The pork-packing business in early Cedar Rapids will always have the claim—along with the mills, factories, and other businesses that once lined the riverfront—of being an important part in the development of business and industry in the city.

to form what is now known as American Federal Savings and Loan Association.

The Perpetual Building and Loan Association had its start on January 28, 1875. It was organized by a small band of officers and employees of the Burlington and Minnesota Railroad, later the Burlington, Cedar Rapids, and Northern. It had no assets when Peter S. Robertson assumed the presidency, but by April 5 had enough money collected to make its first loan of $200. Its growth in assets was slow, but the institution weathered the financial depressions of 1898, 1907, and the 1930s. It did business in a variety of locations in the downtown area, each location reflecting another step in its growth. By the time it moved into its present building in 1957, the association's assets had grown to over $15 million. It has shared in the dramatic economic growth of the 1960s and 1970s.

The third of these early building and loan associations, Valley City Building and Loan, was organized in June 1876, but it did not share in the overall success of the other two. It was lost somewhere in the mists of time; phased out, perhaps, after the initial period of eight years.

Bohemian Savings and Loan was founded in 1892 to service a very limited ethnic customer base. As with Perpetual, it experienced a slow but solid growth up to fairly recent times, then shared the rapid growth of the 1950-1980 period. Reflecting its addition of many banking and financial services and its development of a broad customer base, in June 1984 it changed its name to Banc Iowa and started to operate as a savings bank.

One of the newest and certainly the fastest-growing member of the Cedar Rapids financial community is SCI Financial Group, specializing in investment strategy and investment management. It started out in 1938 as Knapp & Co. under the direction of Russell F. Knapp. In 1948 it became known as Securities Corp. of Iowa, and eventually acquired its present name. With more than $375 million under management in hundreds of portfolios, its subsidiary is believed to be the largest investment firm in the state.

Reflecting the growing needs of a developing area, a number of insurance companies were formed during the 1860s and 1870s. The Farmers Insurance Company was started in 1860 by the Bever and Daniels interests. It appears to have restricted itself to farm property and detached dwellings, which would have exempted it from extraordinary losses through extensive conflagration. In 1921 the considerable

assets of the Farmers Insurance Company were sold to an Eastern insurance group. The Cedar Rapids Insurance Company was organized May 18, 1878, by a group of businessmen headed by Dr. E.L. Mansfield. West Side Fire Insurance was started in 1875 by a James Yuill. Both protected farm buildings and livestock from fire and lightning.

Western Fraternal Life Association is a quiet and unassuming part of the insurance industry of Cedar Rapids. Organized in July 1897 as Western Fraternal Bohemian Association, it was designed for an ethnic customer base, concentrating on fraternal protection and education for its members. It changed to its present name in 1971.

In 1913 a suitcase was transported to Cedar Rapids from Des Moines, and placed in a one-room office. This was the start of the Iowa National Mutual Insurance Company in the city. The firm had been established in 1909 in Des Moines under the name of Automobile Owners Protective Assn. to furnish accident indemnity for liability incurred by reason of maintenance or use of motor vehicles. This was one of the earliest efforts to provide insurance protection for the infant auto industry.

Four years later, all of the records and books of the firm were moved in one suitcase to Cedar Rapids and the firm was set up in a one-room office in the Security Building. In 1914 its name was changed to Iowa Mutual Liability Insurance with a companion company called Iowa Automobile Mutual Insurance Co. that would provide fire coverage on automobiles. By 1936 a change in insurance laws would permit these two companion companies to merge. Its final name, Iowa National Mutual Insurance Company, was adopted in 1950 to reflect further changes in insurance laws.

In the period between 1950 and 1980, the firm saw constant expansion in its business and in its physical plant, resulting in a new headquarters building in 1973 and a 10-story addition in 1980. The early 1980s saw the formation of four new subsidiaries to handle special types of insurance. Employment stood at 900. In 1985 its financial structure suddenly collapsed, and the company was liquidated by the state insurance commissioner.

United Fire and Casualty Company's origin dates back to 1937 when Scott McIntyre, Sr., United's founder, began to gather together small fire and automobile insurance associations into a unified structure. He moved Ace Mutual Insurance Association from Des Moines to Cedar Rapids where the business

Above: Agriculture in Cedar Rapids is more than just a profit-able endeavor. The clean air and natural beauty renew the body and spirit as well. Photo by Craig Aurness. Courtesy, West Light

Above right: Perhaps no other crop is as fitting a symbol for Cedar Rapids as corn, for many years the mainstay of area agriculture. Photo by Craig Aurness. Courtesy, West Light

Right: Since the founding of Cedar Rapids, agribusiness has played a vital role in the economy of the city. Photo by Craig Aurness. Courtesy, West Light

Previous page: A beautiful sunset was captured by photographer Paul Foote

Above: An abandoned farmhouse is a picturesque reminder of Cedar Rapids' early agricultural beginnings. Photo by Paul Foote

Above: The modern skyline is reflected in the river that gave rise to the city. Photo by Paul Foote

Left: The Quaker Oats plant is nearly hidden by the spring blossoms of trees that share its grounds. Photo by Paul Foote

Facing page: A pioneer industry in Cedar Rapids, Quaker Oats has grown to be one of the nation's largest modern companies. The plant is a model of clean industrial efficiency. Photo by Paul Foote

Above, far left: What better way to spend a lazy afternoon than a day of fishing and boating in the calm of a Cedar Rapids lake. Photo by Paul Foote

Above left: Ellis Park is a cool and shady place for quiet reflection. Photo by Paul Foote

Above: The countryside around Cedar Rapids abounds with scenes of the breathtaking beauty that is the harmony of nature. Photo by Paul Foote

Far left: Railroad tracks running through the unspoiled beauty of the countryside outside the city recall a time when Cedar Rapids was the last outpost of the American frontier. Photo by Paul Foote

Left: A park in downtown Cedar Rapids adds natural beauty and a place for a quiet pause in the heart of the city. Photo by Paul Foote

The beauty of a sun-washed spring day is exemplified in the simple juxtaposition of trees, clouds, and a deep blue Iowa sky.
Photo by Paul Foote

was conducted out of one room in the Iowa Theatre building. From that time on, the business was in a constant state of remodeling, building additions, or moving to larger quarters.

In 1938 North Central Mutual Association of Boone was shifted into the Cedar Rapids structure, and the corporate name changed to United Mutual Insurance Association. In 1946 McIntyre organized United Casualty Company, the first casualty insurance company to be organized in Iowa in 25 years. In 1950, when insurance laws were changed to permit multiple line underwriting, the company charter was amended to reflect its current name. During the 1950s additional smaller insurance companies were meshed into the growing structure. Subsidiaries were set up to add life insurance to fire and casualty lines.

The United Fire and Casualty Company today is recognized as one of the most prominent insurance companies in Iowa. It occupies two large buildings on each corner of Second Avenue and Second Street, joined together by an enclosed overhead walkway, a fitting symbol of the activity and success of its founder in joining together insurance operations.

It seems appropriate to close out this chapter with a recap on the meteoric rise of a hometown industry, Life Investors, Inc.

This firm started with an idea—an idea for a life-insurance program to serve Midwesterners—in 1959, with its operations in a 20-by-30-foot office with a desk and telephone in a downtown building. In less than 20 years, Life Investors has become one of the leading life insurance companies in the nation with several billions of dollars of insurance in force.

Today it occupies a vast complex of buildings at Edgewood Road and Forty-second Street N.E. Its growth under dynamic and dedicated leadership has been phenomenal. In 1979 Life Investors became a part of an international investment group when AGO Holding N.V. of Amsterdam acquired control of the company. With new capital for business expansion, its future seems unlimited. It will be an outstanding leader in the second century of the Cedar Rapids insurance industry.

The development of finance and insurance in Cedar Rapids during the past century has been a constant process of entrepreneurship, success and sometimes failure, and service to the community. As it enters its second century, this segment of our business community will face changes with confidence—a confidence gained by its growth and development in the Magnificent Century.

This photograph of the early location and building of Iowa National Mutual Insurance in Cedar Rapids was taken circa 1914.

Above: The home office of the United Fire & Casualty Company in Cedar Rapids. *Courtesy, United Fire & Casualty Company*

Far left: Scott McIntyre, Sr., founder of United Fire & Casualty Company, melded together a unique insurance organization by consolidating smaller insurance companies in the late 1930s. *Courtesy, United Fire & Casualty Company*

Left: Scott McIntyre, Jr., was the second generation of his family to head the United Fire & Casualty Company. *Courtesy, United Fire & Casualty Company*

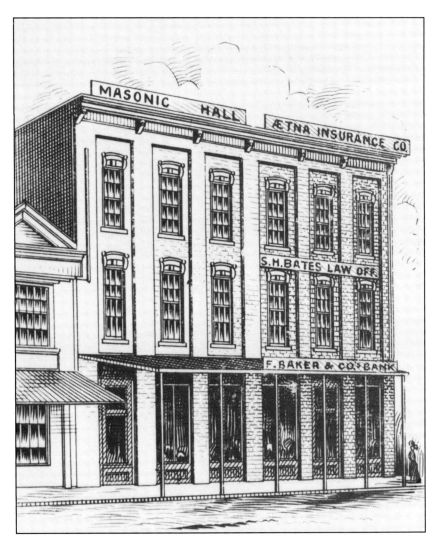

Right: This circa 1870 illustration shows the building that held the early insurance office of Aetna Insurance. It also apparently housed a private bank, a law office, and an early Masonic Hall. From Morcombe, History of Crescent Lodge, 1906

Left: Robert D. Ray, president of Life Investors, Incorporated, and former governor of Iowa. Courtesy, Life Investors, Incorporated

It was at this parade on First Avenue in 1900 that what is believed to be the first photo of automobiles in a parade was made. Courtesy, Iowa Electric Light & Power

TRANSPORTATION

Cedar Rapids has depended upon transportation to sustain and expand its business and industry. At each stage of development, business and industry assessed its current transportation facilities, then set goals for a higher level of transportation, one that would expand enterprise. Each new technological improvement in transportation has had a positive impact upon the economic structure of the city, and, in turn, has become a business or industry in its own right.

When the first settlers of Linn County arrived in the 1840s, their mode of transportation was a nondescript wagon pulled by a pair of reliable but plodding oxen. This was a dependable means of transportation, but certainly not very swift. Once initial settlement was established, the priority of the early farmers and storekeepers was an improved transportation service, one that would get goods to them cheaper and faster, and get the farm products out to a market.

After the arrival of the first steamboat in 1844, the next step in transportation improvement was the stagecoach service put into operation in 1846 by the enterprising Higley brothers. They set up a twice-weekly service between Dubuque, Marion (the county seat), Cedar Rapids, and Iowa City (the state capitol).

The early stages were nothing more than uncovered wagons with one board seat. Passengers were at the mercy of the weather and the streams they had to cross. The schedules were irregular, and the condition of the passengers when they reached their destination was not always good. The ultimate in stagecoach luxury was the Concord coach, but even that left much to be desired. As one passenger described it, the Concord bounced the passengers around like corn popping in a skillet. While fording streams or riding on rough roads, it was not unusual for the coach to overturn and spill everyone out.

After the Higley brothers gave up their stage line, this type of service was handled by the Parker Stage Line, and eventually by Western Stage. The latter was a large stagecoach service which operated in the 1850s and 1860s. In addition to passengers and mail, Western Stage also carried gold and bank currency.

Stagecoach service did not meet all the hopes of the tiny community on the Cedar River.

Above: Stephan Dows was an industrialist, railroad builder, and utility promoter. He arrived in Cedar Rapids in 1855 with a railroad building and engineering background. From Laurance, Pioneer Days In Cedar Rapids, *1936*

Opposite: The Milwaukee railroad depot on First Avenue East is pictured here circa 1900—the Milwaukee trains did not use the Union Depot. This depot remained in service until after World War II. Courtesy, Donald Karr, Jr.

Like every other town of the time, Cedar Rapids desperately wanted a railroad, the very latest in transportation. The railroads had reached Chicago in 1850, and then started to thread lines down to various river points including Rock Island, Fulton, Savannah, and Dubuque.

The Rock Island Railroad reached Iowa City on New Year's Day, 1857. The business leaders of Cedar Rapids and Marion took steps to set up their own railroad line—the Central Iowa Seaboard Air Line—which would connect to the main line at Savannah.

The panic of 1857 brought planning to a halt on this railroad, but another—the Chicago, Iowa, and Nebraska—was starting to build from Clinton. Cedar Rapids leaders went to Clinton to lend their support to the project. Marion leadership, however, stuck to the Savannah route, and there was a cleavage between the two communities on their railroad connections.

The track laid from Clinton cost $18,000 a mile. The business community of Cedar Rapids kept raising money to purchase bonds and stock in the new railroad. The stage line met the railroad as it headed for Cedar Rapids. This provided a one-day service to Chicago, a great step forward in scheduling.

In June 1859 the Chicago, Iowa, and Nebraska Railroad reached Cedar Rapids. Marion waited for its railroad until 1863, when the Dubuque and Southwestern meandered down from Dubuque. This line extended to Cedar Rapids in 1865.

With the railroad came business, and Cedar Rapids became the commercial/industrial center of a multicounty area. The CI&N eventually became part of the Chicago Northwestern Railroad, while the Dubuque and Southwestern merged with the Milwaukee Railroad system.

Still not satisfied with only two railroads, George Greene, Dr. John F. Ely, and other business leaders started the Burlington, Cedar Rapids, and Northern Railroad which eventually stretched from Burlington to Spirit Line, 368 miles of track that became part of the Rock Island in the 1880s. In the meantime, the Illinois Central was building from Dubuque to Council Bluffs, and in 1888 dropped a spur line from Manchester to Cedar Rapids, becoming the fourth railroad to service the city.

Its population, its business, and its industry encouraged tremendous rail service into Cedar Rapids. At the zenith of its rail transportation, around the turn of the century, Cedar Rapids had 73 daily passenger rail schedules in and out of the city. This rail service demanded improved passenger station facilities, and in 1895 Union Station was built.

Interurban rail transportation was implemented shortly after the turn of the century. Electric trolley service was started by Cedar Rapids Power and Light to Iowa City on August 13, 1904. A few years later, trolley service was started between Lisbon and Cedar Rapids, and by 1910 electric train service was operating between Waterloo and Cedar Rapids. These interurbans became thriving businesses, transporting full cars of passengers on frequent and dependable schedules. This unique transportation service ended in the early 1950s, a victim of automobiles and the highway system.

Transportation within the city was not a great problem until the start of the Magnificent Century in 1880. The city limits went only as far as Coe College on 1st Avenue and 12th Street, and most of the residential area of the city extended east to Tenth Street and south to Sixth Avenue. Every part of the city was within walking distance.

In 1879 horse-drawn trolleys in the city connected the short distances between residential areas and downtown. The trolleys were wooden cars drawn by plodding horses or mules with bells attached to them.

In 1880 enterprising George Greene headed a group of businessmen who conceived and started a trolley service between Cedar Rapids and Marion. This single track extended from the railroad track on

First Avenue to Marion. The steam-driven trolley wheezed and smoked all the way, causing no end of havoc and ire in the big homes that lined First Avenue all the way to Coe College. Homeowners' complaints caused the city council to rule that the trolley car had to be horse-drawn up to Coe College, after which it could use its engine.

The horse-drawn trolleys operated until 1891 when electricity was used to power this form of transportation. The electric trolleys served the city very well. Their routes were continually extended as the city grew, and their fare was very reasonable—five cents. They connected the far reaches of the city—Bever Park in the southeast with the Alamo Amusement Park in the northwest—and all areas in between. These streetcars were hardly more than open cars with electric motors. Some of them had coal heaters for use during the winter.

By the mid-1930s there was considerable public pressure to replace the antiquated trolley car system with a modern bus system. On November 14, 1937, a bus system replaced the trolley car system. The Marion express made its last wheezing journey on November 13, 1937. An era had ended.

The novelty of the electric streetcars had hardly worn off when in 1895 news of the "horseless carriage" reached Cedar Rapids. In less than 50 years, the sale, servicing, and maintenance of these "horseless carriages" would become a substantial business in the city and would cause the demise of the railroad system.

In 1899 the calm of the Cedar Rapids streets was broken by a steam Locomobile brought into town by a young coal dealer, W.G. Haskell. This would be followed in 1900 by two internal-combustion automobiles operated by Clarence Miller, copublisher of the *Gazette,* and by Colonel William Downs, an industrialist.

The advent of the automobile caused many problems in the city. The city council passed a variety of ordinances to regulate or discourage their use. The Cedar Rapids Commercial Club, meanwhile, tried unsuccessfully to get an automobile manufacturer to locate in the city. In 1902 Cedar Rapids had its first automobile dealer, F.W. Weaver, who had to locate his shop outside of the city limits. A few years later, the Lattner brothers, Joe and P.M., set up a dealership on Fourth Avenue and Third Street S.E.

During the World War I era, this new method of transportation developed into a business of its own. Dealers for Packards, Cadillacs, Fords, Peerless,

Buicks, and dozens of other brands set up their places of business. Automobile service businesses were started in conjunction with dealerships. Rapids Chevrolet and automobile dealers such as Allens became substantial members of the business community. The 1930s saw more dealerships arrive—Baxter, Langhurst, Schamberger, Culver, and Rude.

The 1930s also saw the motor truck become a vital part of the freight transportation system, not only in Cedar Rapids but also across the entire country. Trucking companies became a factor in the daily transportation of products in and out of Cedar Rapids, and truck terminals became a part of the business scene. By the 1940s and 1950s these terminals were transportation centers and warehouses, spots where merchandise was brought in and transported out.

As the automobile became popular, Cedar Rapids business leaders began to assess the highway system in Linn County.

The "good roads" movement in the county was spearheaded by two energetic business leaders, W.G. Haskell and Ed Killian. Haskell had introduced the steam Locomobile into Cedar Rapids in 1899 and was an avid auto fan. Killian, founder of a department store, wanted people in rural areas to be able to come into the city to shop.

Haskell and Killian co-chaired a local committee that in 1918 persuaded the Linn County Board of Supervisors to appropriate $2,100 for a "seedling mile" of cement along Highway 30 between Cedar Rapids and Mount Vernon. The Northwestern States Portland Cement Company of Mason City provided the cement for this project. This first mile of cement highway spurred popular support for a bond that began a highway-paving program in the county. The improved highway system expanded the immediate trade territory of the city, laid the foundation for the trucking industry, expanded the automobile sales/ service business, and, in the 1960s, spurred the completion of I-380.

While automobiles were being improved and the highway system was being modernized, the businesses and people of Cedar Rapids were realizing that another mode of transportation would be available in the future.

The first airplane in Cedar Rapids was operated by an ex-World War I pilot, Dan Hunter, in a pasture on the south edge of the city. With a makeshift hangar and a plane that he maintained himself, Hunter performed an aerial circus act for county fairs, did special barnstorming promotions, gave flight instruction to would-be pilots, and was available for emergency chartered flights. His runway was not very long, and it was only grass and dirt. This patchwork operation spurred local interest in aviation.

Boeing Air Transport started using the Hunter field in 1928 on its government mail shuttle between Chicago and San Francisco. Boeing also provided limited passenger service for a time, but only under ideal weather conditions. When a bond to provide an all-weather runway was defeated in 1929, Boeing discontinued its services. In the late 1930s Hunter used his field for government pilot-training programs and Coe College used it for its War Training Program.

World War II and a large dose of civic pride prompted Cedar Rapids to enter the age of modern aviation in 1942. After Pearl Harbor, airports and airfields became a top priority in Congress, and appropriations were made to develop 250 civilian airports. Cedar Rapids business and city officials set their sights on securing a Class 4 airport facility, one that would have runways capable of handling large aircraft. The government would pay for the construction of such fields if the city would provide the land. A $325,000 bond issue was passed to buy land for such an airport, the Civil Aeronautics Commission was successfully petitioned for such a facility, and 640 acres of land south of the city was purchased. The airport runways were started in 1943, and the farmhouse on the tract was used for a makeshift terminal.

World War II ended without the new airport being used for military purposes. Cedar Rapids business and industrial leaders then pushed for a commercial airport. After 22 hearings in Washington, Cedar Rapids' airport was included on the regular schedule of United Airlines. The first regularly scheduled United flight at the Cedar Rapids airport arrived on April 27, 1947, as a DC-3 Mainliner touched the 5,400-foot runway. Cedar Rapids was now a part of the air age.

With the airport the business and industry of Cedar Rapids entered a new era in development. The city was now linked with all parts of the world. Sales representatives from industrial, electronic, and technological firms traveled all over the world selling products from the city. The export business of Cedar Rapids increased dramatically when the airport started air-cargo shipments.

Business, industry, and the people of Cedar Rapids pressed for a terminal building that would complement the modern runways and also symbolize the economic vitality of the city. The new terminal, open by 1953, had numerous additions and renovations during the next 20 years as it kept pace with the ever-increasing freight and passenger volume. Air transportation service and facilities were vital to the tremendous industrial expansion that Cedar Rapids experienced in the 1950s, when Downing Box, General Mills, Corn Sweeteners, and many other

Above: This crowd witnessed the departure of the first passenger flight from Cedar Rapids airport on April 27, 1947. The farmhouse was converted for use as the terminal building for five years, until a new terminal could be built.

Opposite: Clarence Miller, co-owner of the Cedar Rapids Gazette, *was photographed circa 1901 in one of the first automobiles in Cedar Rapids. These first automobiles, lever-guided, were quite a sensation in the city. Courtesy, Peoples Bank & Trust Co.*

industries located their massive plants in the city.

In the late 1970s it became increasingly evident that either a massive renovation/expansion of the present terminal or a completely new terminal was necessary. The export business in 1960 was $29 million; in 1979 it was approaching $450 million. Air cargo, the first year the airport was in operation, had been 114,000 pounds; air freight handled in 1979 was 8,426,800 pounds. During the first year of operation, 5,000 passengers had passed through the makeshift terminal; in 1979 the passenger count was 509,827.

A decision was made to build a new terminal. That was the easy part. It took several years to finalize the design and to arrive at a satisfactory cost level, but eventually terminal construction was underway. The new terminal was dedicated on October 21, 1986, a fitting end to a century of transportation progress.

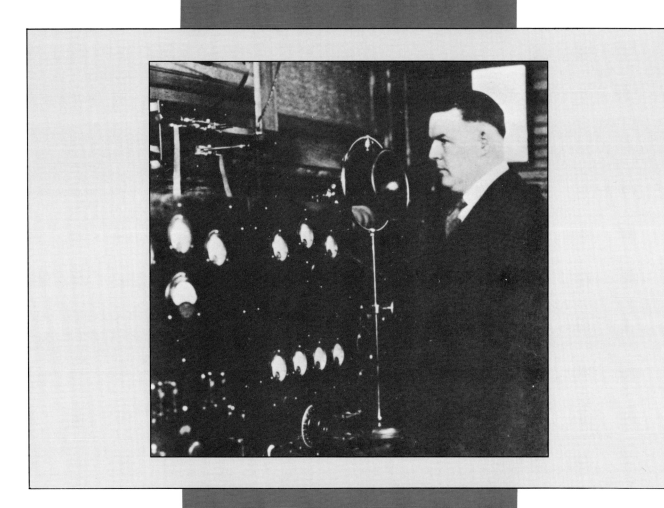

Douglas M. Perham is pictured here using a carbon transmitter in one of the first broadcasts of radio station WJAM in 1922. The call letters were later changed to WMT. The broadcasts emanated from the top floor of a westside garage. From Clements, Tales of the Town, *1967*

COMMUNICATIONS
AND
ELECTRONICS

The communications industry in Cedar Rapids began in 1851 when D.O. Finch published the city's first newpaper, *The Progressive Era.* Like all early newspapermen, Finch used a hand press and set his type by hand. It was a standard four-page weekly, and from all accounts was not a bad paper.

Publishing a newspaper in those days was a lonely and chancy job. The publisher had to run the business, help with the press, edit, and solicit advertising. Finch soon tired of this and sold the paper. The paper went through a series of owners, and eventually became the *Cedar Rapids Times.* Another newspaper, the *Cedar Rapids Democrat,* started in 1856 but lasted only about three years.

The next 30 years saw dozens of newspapers started in the city, most of them only surviving a year or so. The exception to this was the *Cedar Rapids Republican,* which started printing as a daily on September 1, 1870. It survived until 1927 when it was taken over by the *Gazette.*

In late 1882, two men with previous newspaper experience came to Cedar Rapids from Illinois. They were L.H. Post and E.L. Otis. Encountering stiff competition from existing publications, the *Evening Gazette* started out on January 10, 1883, at 309 First Avenue with 1,200 papers daily. It was rough going. Otis lost his enthusiasm in six months and returned to Illinois. Post stuck it out for another nine months, but his chances for survival looked bleak. Collections were lagging, advertising was hard to sell, and expenses kept growing.

Post found two men in the community interested in the paper, Clarence L. Miller and Fred Faulkes. Post took them into partnership, with Miller managing the business affairs and Faulkes editing and turning out the paper. This arrangement lasted for three months, then Post abruptly left. Miller and Faulkes reorganized the paper and kept it going. They did a good job of it. Over 100 years later, the paper is still here.

Development of the *Gazette* continued to be guided by representatives of the Miller and Faulkes families until 1914 when a composing-room employee, Harry L. Marshall, became the third partner in the business. The growth of the paper necessitated frequent moves to larger quarters until 1925 when it moved to its present site.

The *Gazette* was awarded the Pulitzer Prize in 1936 for "distinguished and meritorious public

Above left: J.L. Enos was editor of the New Era, *the first newspaper in Cedar Rapids, established in 1851. From Morcombe,* History of Crescent Lodge, *1906*

Above right: Fred W. Faulkes was co-publisher of the Cedar Rapids Gazette *when it started publication in 1883. He manned the editorial desk, while his partner, Clarence Miller, was the business manager. From Murray,* Story of Cedar Rapids, *1950*

Opposite: Greene's Opera House, pictured here circa 1890, was built in 1880 by George Greene, and hosted the finest national and international talent. This facility was considered the finest opera house between Chicago and Denver. It operated as a vaudeville house until the 1920s. From Clements, Tales of the Town, *1967*

service in journalism." This continues to be its motto.

A few years after the newspaper business was established, another forward step was made in improving communication. This step came in late 1859 when the Cedar Rapids and Missouri River Telegraph Company started to provide service to Cedar Rapids. Now business and industry had direct and fast contact with enterprise throughout the country.

The communication industry of Cedar Rapids progressed one step more on November 22, 1877, when a new-fangled gadget—the telephone—was demonstrated. One of Alexander Graham Bell's associates, P.D. Richards, had come to Cedar Rapids to show off the new device.

Richards hooked up two telephones by a direct line between the Pope and Ballau drugstore and the Waite Music Store. Both of these stores were on First Avenue between First and Second streets. The business community, while it did not understand the mechanics of the telephone, knew it would become an essential.

Two local young men, George C. Engle and David Holt Ogden, also realized its potential. Pooling their resources and background in telegraphy, they would help establish permanent telephone service in Cedar Rapids. They organized George C. Engle and Company in 1878 to set up lines in the business section of the city and to build a telephone exchange panel.

George C. Engle and Company became the

GRADING AND ROAD-MAKING MACHINERY

The "good roads" movement of the early 1900s launched another industry in Cedar Rapids—the grading and road-making machinery industry.

The emergence of this industry came at an opportune time. Around 1910 the economic structure of the city was in a state of transition, a "sputtering" stage. Its old, established businesses were disappearing from the scene, victims of time and circumstance. It no longer had its farm-implement factories, soap factories, clothing factories, barrel factories, sawmills, or breweries. This economic void had to be filled by increased retail-wholesale-service businesses and by new types of industries. Into this void came the grading and road-machinery industries.

The pioneer manufacturer of this type of machinery in Cedar Rapids was the Universal Engineering Company, originally known as the Universal Crusher Company. It was founded in 1906 on a patented "jaw crusher," which utilized an overhead eccentric shaft. For many years this type of crusher was the only one of its kind in the road-building industry. The jaw crusher had been designed and patented by a mechanical genius, John Valdy, who interested a group of investors, including Robert Sinclair of the Sinclair packing house family, in financing the company.

With production headquarters in a nondescript building at 508 F Avenue N.W., the company started to turn out a line of commercial rock crushers that could be used in road building. The manufacturing operation was shifted to several larger facilities until a new office and plant facility was erected in 1924 at 625 C Avenue N.W.

When automobiles began to outpace the horse as a main mode of transportation, Universal's business soared. Faster cars caused a great consumer demand for adequately paved roads. In response to this demand, Universal designed and produced a portable crusher with a high reduction ratio that enabled contractors to make use of roadside quarries and pits rather than attempt to transport crushed material from commercial plants. This concept of portable crushers revolutionized the road-building industry.

The Great Depression slowed the road-building industry almost to a halt. Universal survived the Depression, and during World War II geared itself to producing ordnance devices

Top: A 1930 photo of LaPlant-Choate Manufacturing Company at First Avenue east. This facility produced dump wagons, snow plows, bulldozers, and trailers. Courtesy, Cedar Rapids Chamber of Commerce

Bottom left: Roy E. Choate and his uncle, E.W. LaPlant, in the early 1900s formed the LaPlant-Choate Manufacturing Company. An accomplished engineer, Choate distinguished himself in the grading and road-making machinery field. He was president of the Chamber of Commerce in 1940. Courtesy, Cedar Rapids Chamber of Commerce

Bottom right: E.W. LaPlant started LaPlant-Choate Manufacturing Company in 1899 as a house-moving operation. He took his nephew, Roy Choate, into the firm in the early 1900s and expanded its operations.

for the armed forces. The company name was changed to Universal Engineering to reflect the war products added to the crusher line, and it received an "E" Award for wartime production. Postwar reconversion brought the company back to its primary line of crushers and related products.

In 1948 the Pettibone Mulliken Corporation of Chicago purchased the company, operating it as a wholly owned subsidiary. The period 1950-1980 saw a tremendous growth of international markets for rock crushers and asphalt-mixing plants. This overseas market became a major source of revenue for the company. Emphasis on the export market cushioned the company against the peaks and valleys of the domestic business, but it also had its perils. The fluctuation of the international market since 1980 had its effect on the construction-equipment industry in general, and, in turn, upon Universal.

In early 1986 Pettibone Mulliken and its subsidiaries filed for reorganization under Chapter 11. Universal officials are hopeful that the reorganization can be successfully completed in the near future.

The LaPlant-Choate Manufacturing Company was another early pioneer in the development of modern road machinery. In its day, it was the largest manufacturer of earth-moving and land-clearing equipment in the world. Among its many and varied products were hydraulic and cable-controlled bulldozers, trail builders, tree dozers and scrapers, and a complete line of land-clearing tools.

The beginnings of LaPlant-Choate started in the early 1900s when Roy E. Choate, a young engineer, moved to Cedar Rapids to associate himself in the house-moving business with his uncle, E.W. LaPlant. LaPlant had started his business in 1899, using only an old horse and a box of tools. He used collar rollers, but was continually experimenting with wheeled trucks to put under the houses.

Together LaPlant and Choate developed house-moving trucks. They eventually manufactured these trucks and sold them nationwide. In 1908 they developed a stump puller, and decided to form the LaPlant-Choate Manufacturing Company. Their original plant was located near the site of the present McKinley School. The business went well, and in 1914 they conceived the idea of the earth scraper and commenced manufacturing it. They also turned out a line of oil field trailers used to transport pipe through the mud of the oil fields.

World War I was the proving ground for the track-type tractor that could be used to transport big guns. LaPlant-Choate was not long in adapting this track-tractor concept to their earth scrapers, and by 1920 they were building huge earth wagons for the construction of the Hoover and Grand Coulee dams. About this time, they moved into a new building at First Avenue East and Thirteenth Street.

In the 1930s the company added a line of tractor-drawn tree dozers. This equipment was particularly useful in southern Texas where there were millions of acres of uncleared land. Large dump wagons and heavy-duty wagons were also added to their line.

With the coming of World War II, LaPlant-Choate started to build dozers for military use, producing 38 percent of all dozers used by the armed forces. The most famous of all the company's war tools was the tankdozer. Given priority handling, this tankdozer was conceived and engineered by Roy Choate and his engineering staff in just a few days. Mounted on the M-4 tank, these tankdozers were responsible for breaching the hedgerows in Normandy after the invasion in 1944. The navy used these same dozers to demolish Japanese pillboxes. LaPlant-Choate received widespread publicity for the part its bulldozers played in the war.

After the war, technology and engineering continued to be a priority at LaPlant-Choate, and the self-loading scraper was developed. However, these were years of declining sales and poor earnings. In 1952 the company was sold to Allis Chalmers Manufacturing Company of Milwaukee, Wisconsin.

In 1968 the company moved into a new 300,000-square-foot facility in the southwest quadrant of the city. That year also heard the first rumblings that

the Allis Chalmers empire was in trouble. Its profits were plummeting, as were its estimated sales and earnings. There were numerous corporate takeover attempts, and drastic steps had to be taken to reverse the profit decline. Employment and production restructuring was vital. In November 1968 the new Cedar Rapids plant was closed, and the company shifted production to Springfield and Deerfield, Illinois. In 1969 Harnischfeger Corporation of Milwaukee took over all existing personnel and facilities, and phased in its new hydraulic equipment lines.

Although the 1970s were years of success for Harnischfeger, the 1980s brought domestic and international decline in the construction-machinery industry. On May 30, 1986, the company announced it had no alternative but to phase out its Cedar Rapids plant. This phasing-out has now reached its conclusion.

The Speeder Machinery Company emerged on the Cedar Rapids industrial scene in 1926. It had moved its employees and its business en masse from Fairfield, Iowa, where it had been located since 1922.

The company had started out in Leon, Iowa, in 1919. G.T. Ronk decided to build a machine that would load piles of gravel from the roadside into other vehicles. To do this, Ronk combined a 15-horsepower, two-cycle gasoline engine, a chain drive linked to wheels on a hay wagon, ropes driven by a form of winch, and a tumblebug bucket holding about a yard of material. The machine worked, and worked well. Ronk found financing for his invention in Fairfield, and moved the business there in 1922.

At the time of the move to Fairfield, the manufacturing equipment consisted of two lathes, a drill press, a power saw, and a forge. In the next four years, about 100 machines were built and sold. By 1926 the annual sales of Speeder Machinery had reached 80 machines. It had outgrown its plant, and Fairfield was unable to meet the demands of the company's growth and its labor needs. At this point the company moved to Cedar Rapids, occupying a site at 1201 Sixth Street S.W.

In 1939 Ronk sold the company to Link Belt Company of Chicago, who merged its crane division with the Speeder Machinery Company to form the Link Belt-Speeder Corporation, a wholly owned subsidiary of the Link Belt Company. This merger resulted in a complete line of cranes and excavators. The business continued to flourish, and in 1957 a sizable addition was constructed to the original plant. In 1966 two more buildings were added on a site on Bowling Street S.W.

Above: Mounted on crawler wheels and equipped as a dragline, this was one of the models turned out by Speeder Machinery circa 1930. Courtesy, Donald Karr, Jr.

Opposite: Howard Hall, pictured here in 1968, was instrumental in the industrial development surge of the 1950s, 1960s, and 1970s. Hall was the founder of the Iowa Manufacturing Company in 1923, now known as Cedar Rapids, Incorporated. Courtesy, Cedar Rapids Gazette

In June 1967 the Link Belt Company was acquired by FMC Corporation, an international organization engaged in producing a wide variety of machinery and chemical products. In 1973 the name Link Belt-Speeder was changed to Crane and Excavator Division of FMC. Under FMC operation, the local plant enjoyed a high tide of prosperity in the 1970s. In March 1978 an additional 91 acres was purchased on Bowling Street for a new engineering building. Employment hit a peak of 2,300.

In the early part of 1980, as in the case of Universal Engineering and Harnischfeger, the company began to feel the effects of a depressed domestic and international market for heavy-construction equipment. Layoffs and corporate uneasiness prevailed from 1981 through 1984. On February 21, 1985, FMC officials made the reluctant announcement that production would cease in the Cedar Rapids plant.

Iowa Manufacturing Company arrived on the grading and road-making scene in Cedar Rapids in 1923. It was the creation of one man, Howard Hall, and it continued to be directed by him until his death on

May 16, 1971. A native of Onslow, Iowa, Hall had worked for a Cedar Rapids bank until 1917 when he joined the army and served with the American Expeditionary Forces in France. Returning to civilian life in 1919, Hall purchased an interest in Iowa Steel and Iron Works, becoming its president in 1922. In 1923 he organized the Iowa Manufacturing Company.

With the road-building programs getting under way, Hall purchased the small Bertschey Engineering Company machine shop and began to convert it into a factory for building rock-crushing, screening, and conveying machinery. Rock-crushing equipment for road building in those days was stationary and difficult to move without extensive dismantling. Because of this, the construction of hard surfaced roads was a slow and expensive process. The need was sorely felt for a wheel-mounted machine that could be transported directly to a quarry or gravel deposit near the road project.

To solve this problem, Iowa Manufacturing Company offered a portable crushing, screening, and load-

ing plant—the first one-piece unit on the market. This became available in the mid-1920s and was an instant success.

Iowa Manufacturing continued to develop a line of road-building machinery consisting of a series of units calculated to care for every aggregate-reducing and handling problem. The company could engineer a plant to meet any requirement of size or quality without the cost of special equipment.

Under Hall's direction, the product line of Iowa Manufacturing was never stagnant. In 1929 the company marketed its first asphalt plant. These asphalt-mixing plants became the top of the line in the business. In 1956 an asphalt paver was introduced.

Following Hall's death in 1971, Iowa Manufacturing became a subsidiary of the Raytheon Company headquartered in Lexington, Massachusetts. During the 1970s, like the rest of the construction-machinery industry, it developed a sizable international market, but it also continued to build up a solid domestic market. The company has weathered well the current depression in the construction-machinery industry. It continues to develop new product lines and shows great promise for the future.

The company's trademark, "Cedarapids," has always been on its machines and has become very well known nationally and internationally. On July 8, 1985, the company name was changed from Iowa Manufacturing Company to Cedarapids, Inc.

The last of the road-machinery manufactures in Cedar Rapids was started in the 1940s by Roy Gaddis. The Highway Equipment Company specialized in sand, salt, lime, and fertilizer spreaders, mostly truck-mounted. It was operated by the Gaddis family until 1957 when it was sold to Clifford H. Jordan, a Cedar Rapids businessman. In July 1978 the firm was purchased by two of its executive officers, C.M. Basile and W.T. Rissi.

The company manufactures a complete line of spreaders for highway use, such as aggregate spreaders, sand and gravel spreaders, and agricultural lime and fertilizer spreaders. These machines can also be used for putting a seal coating on top of newly laid oil, spreading sand and cinders for ice control, and spreading powdered chlorine for dust control.

The grading and road-making machinery industry in Cedar Rapids filled a void in the economic structure of the city at the turn of the century. Since then it has made an important contribution to Cedar Rapids' economic structure, and will continue to do so in the future.

Top left: The Longview Fibre plant on Blair's Ferry Road N.E. was built in 1956, the year this photograph was taken, for Downing Box Company. Downing Box was acquired by Longview Fibre in the late 1970s. Courtesy, Cedar Rapids Chamber of Commerce

Bottom left: MGD Graphic Systems in southwest Cedar Rapids is a division of North American Rockwell. Erected in 1965, this plant produces Metroliner printing presses. Courtesy, Cedar Rapids Chamber of Commerce

Right: This circa 1950 photograph shows the first production facilities of Nissen Trampoline Company at 200 A Avenue N.W. Courtesy, Cedar Rapids Chamber of Commerce

THE FABULOUS '50s AND '60s INDUSTRIES

The period between 1950 and 1980 was a fabulous era in the business and industrial growth of Cedar Rapids. It could almost be labeled the "Golden Thirty Years" of Cedar Rapids.

It was during this time, particularly the 1950s and 1960s, that Cedar Rapids was pinpointed in many industrial planning maps in the executive offices of national corporations. The strategic location of Cedar Rapids, coupled with its rural manpower reserves, made it attractive to all types of industry and business. This period in Cedar Rapids saw the blossoming of already existing industries like LeFebure Corporation, Dearborn Brass, Midland Industries, and Cedar Rapids Engineering. It also saw the acquisition of new and exciting industries such as Nissen Trampoline, Cryovac, Square D. Downing Box, Goss Company, J-Tec, and Norand. General Mills and Corn Sweeteners emerged on the industrial scene in the late 1970s.

The 1950s and the 1960s also saw the emergence of the Chamber of Commerce as a significant factor in the economic and industrial development of the community. The Chamber of Commerce, in one form or another, had been on the scene since 1880. At that time it was known as the Cedar Rapids Board of Trade. It and its successor, the Cedar Rapids Commercial Club, had been primarily a businessmen's organization, dedicated to improving the business climate of the city, and to making the city a better place to live in. In 1917 the Commercial Club was replaced by the Cedar Rapids Chamber of Commerce.

All of these organizations were relatively static as far as economic/industrial development was concerned. Most of their time was occupied with the internal welfare of the city, rather than the external merchandising of the city for industrial and business expansion. It remained for the "Golden Thirty Years" to produce a Chamber of Commerce geared to intensive promotion of the city.

The Cedar Rapids Board of Trade was nearing its end in 1892 when Emil T. LeFebure founded the LeFebure Corporation. LeFebure, a native of Belgium, had immigrated to the United States in 1859. By 1892 he was located in Cedar Rapids where he started a bindery that produced self-indexing ledgers for business accounting. His first quarters were at 119 First Street S.W.

By 1905 the LeFebure Ledger Company, as it was known then, had become the largest

Above: LeFebure Corporation's plant at 308 Twenty-ninth Street N.E. provides jobs for around 1,500 people. The facility produces electronic banking equipment, bank vault doors, safe deposit boxes, bank security devices, and related items. Courtesy, Cedar Rapids Chamber of Commerce

Below left: Nate Cohn, executive vice president of Dearborn Brass in the 1960s, also served as a director of the Cedar Rapids Chamber of Commerce. From Dearborn Brass, Three Quarters of a Century, *1971*

Below right: Ed Cohn served as president of Dearborn Brass during the 1960s when it was recognized as one of the world's largest manufacturers of tubular brass fittings. From Dearborn Brass, Three Quarters of a Century, *1971*

bindery in Cedar Rapids. Its product, the "X-ray ledger," was shipped to many areas of the country. Emil LeFebure lost control of the company in 1909, but his son, Leo T. LeFebure, remained with the company and subsequently regained control of it.

The company name was changed to LeFebure Corporation in 1938, reflecting a broadened product line. However, until 1955 the primary product of the firm remained accounting books and record-keeping materials. At this time the plant was occupying a large old building at 716 Oakland Avenue N.E.

In early 1956 Leo LeFebure sold the business to Craig Systems of Danvers, Massachusetts, who consolidated the company into its production of cycle billing systems for department stores and banking systems. It was after this consolidation that LeFebure entered into the production of metal concealed security equipment for bank-teller stations. This was the start of broad product development.

Sales and production capabilities increased rapidly. The Cedar Rapids division grew to account for a major part of the parent company's volume and earnings. To reflect this situation, the parent company eventually took the name of the subsidiary.

The LeFebure Corporation left its old building on Oakland Avenue in 1960 and moved to the former Fruehauf Trailer plant on Twenty-eighth Street and First Avenue N.E. Expansion of this plant commenced almost immediately. Additions to the production line included vault doors and safe-deposit boxes plus other types of bank equipment.

In 1966 LeFebure attracted the attention of the Walter L. Kidde Company of New Jersey, at that time the largest producer of safety and security equipment in the world. The Cedar Rapids operation became an autonomous division of the parent company. It had a major plant addition in 1968 to make room for an expanded line of products. Another multimillion-dollar expansion followed in 1973.

Kidde sold five of its subsidiaries, including LeFebure, in 1985 to L.B. Foster, Inc., of Pittsburgh. The company is still a part of Foster. At the time of this sale, LeFebure had 1,500 employees and was recognized as a leading producer of electronic banking equipment, bank vault doors, chests, safe-deposit boxes, bank security devices, drive-up banking systems, and depositories. It was a substantial corporate citizen of the community.

In 1896, four years after Emil LeFebure started his accounting ledger business in Cedar Rapids, another industry that would make its mark on Cedar Rapids sprang up on Dearborn Street in Chicago.

Fred Erickson and Louis Kruber founded the Dearborn Brass Manufacturing Company in 1896. In 1901 they moved operations and personnel to a small machine shop in Cedar Rapids at 805 B Avenue N.W. Their main products were nickel-plated faucets and brass fittings.

Esac Cohn, founder of the local E. Cohn and Sons, a scrap-metal firm, acquired control of the Dearborn Brass operation in 1926. The Cohn family operated the scrap-iron business, Dearborn Brass, and Cedar Rapids Pump and Supply as independent businesses with family members in charge of each. Under the Cohn family, Dearborn Brass continued to expand until, in the late 1960s, it was recognized as one of the world's largest manufacturers of tubular-brass fittings. It supplied plumbing wholesalers with brass traps, sink and bathtub waste traps, wall and yard hydrants, brass valves and hose faucets, shower curtain rods and accessories, basket sink strainers, and related plumbing products.

Dearborn was acquired by Beatrice Foods of Chicago in 1972. The firm continued to expand its line of products, its sales, and its local facilities. A new plant was opened on Shaver Road N.E. In 1975 the firm was given the Community Recognition Award, cited as the largest consumer of wrought brass in the Midwest. It had subsidiary plants in Denver and in Tyler, Texas.

In the late 1970s the advent of plastic plumbing and aging facilities caught up with Dearborn Brass. Operations were concentrated on production at the Denver and Tyler facilities. In March 1981 the Cedar Rapids operation was closed down, ending an 80-year relationship with the city. In its day and its time, Dearborn Brass had served well the economic structure of Cedar Rapids.

Another industry that blossomed in the 1950s and 1960s was Cedar Rapids Engineering Company, now known as Kwik-Way Corporation. It got its start in 1920 by providing a product badly needed by the automobile and trucking industry: a reliable valve-facing machine. Until this machine was marketed, valve facing was a difficult process that had to be done by hand.

The founders of Cedar Rapids Engineering were Charles C. Hahn, a former blacksmith's apprentice who loved automobiles and wanted to solve some of their problems, and Richard H. Meister, a skilled mechanic and machinist. Between them, they designed the much-needed machine. Their modest office and shop at 902 Seventeenth Street N.E. was soon busy turning out these new machines. Their traveling sales-

men traversed the dusty roads of Iowa, Nebraska, and North and South Dakota selling these valve-facing machines, primarily to garages. The business enjoyed steady success.

During World War II the company devoted its machining skills to grinding radio crystals. After the war Cedar Rapids Engineering turned its attention increasingly to foreign markets, and by 1962 it was selling directly to overseas customers.

The Hahn family continued to direct the company until 1968 when it was merged into Kwik-Way Industries, and a new professional management team was formed. Kwik-Way rapidly expanded its service and sales, acquiring several other firms in allied manufacturing.

By 1974 the company had outgrown its Seventeenth Street facilities, enlarged as much as possible by continued expansions, and decided to relocate on the east side of Marion, where suitable industrial land was available. Located on a 20-acre site, the plant was occupied in early 1976. The new plant made possible an expansion of product lines, and employment reached almost 300. By 1981 it was necessary to add 30 percent to the production facilities to turn out a new product—the Kwik-lathe, used for machining front-wheel drive disc brakes.

The company continues to respond to changes in technology. Today it has long-range plans to expand its lines in engine reconditioning and brake-repair equipment.

The World War II era saw practically all of Cedar Rapids' industry producing the materials and products needed for the war effort. Midland Industries, now known as Midland Forge, got its start in 1943 turning out steel shackles to sell to the government. The firm was organized by Don M. McIntyre. After the war the same shackles were sold to farmers for use as clevises. Shackles and clevises still remain a basic part of the business, although its product line has been expanded.

The company operated out of an old building at 910 Second Avenue S.W. throughout the war and postwar years. McIntyre eventually sold the business to Ellis G. Cram who operated it until 1972 when ill health forced him to sell it to C.P. Rohde.

Rohde analyzed the operation and the facilities, assessed its potential, and made some changes that made the company an essential part of the "Golden Thirty Years" of Cedar Rapids' industrial development and growth. He changed the name to Midland Forge, then erected a new plant at 101 Fiftieth Avenue S.W.

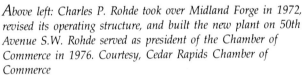

Above left: Charles P. Rohde took over Midland Forge in 1972, revised its operating structure, and built the new plant on 50th Avenue S.W. Rohde served as president of the Chamber of Commerce in 1976. Courtesy, Cedar Rapids Chamber of Commerce

Above right: George Nissen founded the Nissen Trampoline Company in 1935 and guided it into the 1960s when it was recognized as the world's largest manufacturer of gymnastic equipment. Nissen is also an outstanding gymnast.

Opposite: Cryovac Division's W.R. Grace Plant, on Wilson Avenue S.W., has undergone several additions since this photograph was taken in 1952. The plant produces plastic bags. Photo by Thompson Photographers. Courtesy, Cedar Rapids Chamber of Commerce

Located on a 15-acre site, the 46,000-square-foot plant was considered at the time to be the most modern steel-forging plant in the country.

The plant was sold in 1976 to Columbus McKinnon Corporation of Tonawanda, New York, one of the world's leading manufacturers of chain and hoists. Today it continues to expand its product lines.

The Nissen Trampoline Company, now known as Nissen/Universal, started in 1935 when a young American tumbling and diving champion, George Nissen, cleared out his father's garage and used a bed frame to build his first trampoline. In 1946 the Nissen Trampoline Company opened for business at 200 A Avenue N.W.

Nissen's product won immediate acceptance, and the first national collegiate trampoline champion, crowned in 1948, was using a Nissen trampoline. By 1964 trampolining was being organized internationally, and the Cedar Rapids Nissen trampoline was in demand all over the world.

In 1959 the company erected a plant in a new industrial park in the southwest quadrant of the city. The new plant permitted Nissen to produce a line of high-quality gymnasium equipment in the 1960s, to supplement their line of trampolines. This equipment included parallel bars and balance beams, tumbling and

wrestling mats, electric scoreboards, and basketball backstops. By the end of the 1960s, the company was the world's largest manufacturer of gymnastic apparatus.

The following years saw Nissen acquiring several smaller manufacturers of sporting goods. In turn Nissen was looked upon as a possible merger by larger firms such as Wilson Sporting Goods. In 1972 Nissen was acquired by Victor Comptometer Corp. as a subsidiary.

Walter Kidde, Inc., purchased the company in 1978. Kidde also bought Universal Gym Equipment, and combined the two into one operation. Additional production facilities have enabled the company in recent years to branch out into electronic bikes, treadmills, and electronic message panels.

In early 1948, a couple of years after George Nissen started to make trampolines, the Chamber of Commerce secured the services of a young and energetic organization executive, a professional in his field, Robert H. Caldwell. Caldwell correctly analyzed the potential business leadership in Cedar Rapids and its latent community assets. He assembled economic and demographic data. He established contact with railroad industrial departments, factory-locating services, and the Iowa Development Commission. He set up a

system of direct-mailings to known prospects and to firms that the chamber wanted to interest in the city. He structured the business leadership into industrial development committees, then waited for the opportune time to use these community assets and reserves. It was not long in coming.

In 1951 the Dewey and Almy Chemical Company, an Eastern-based corporation, was looking for a Midwestern site to erect a plant to manufacture Cryovac plastic bags. Letters had been sent out to about 450 Chambers of Commerce throughout the Midwest to gather information on water supply, land transportation, taxes, and labor availability.

When the questionnaires were returned and evaluated, Cedar Rapids and four other cities were chosen for consideration. Cedar Rapids won in the selection process. It was close to the country's leading meat packer, and it was the geographic center of much of the company's existing distribution area. The advance delegation was also impressed with the civic pride of the city, the cooperative attitude of its city government and business leaders, the friendliness of its people, and its facilities.

In a short time, ground was broken for a 76,000-square-foot plant, a plant that would receive numerous additions through the years—1953, 1954, 1957,

1958, and 1967—until it would be double its original size. In 1954 Dewey and Almy became a division of W.R. Grace Company, and in 1956 Cyrovac was made a separate division. Its production volume continues to increase each year.

The next industrial opportunity for Cedar Rapids came in 1954 when Square D Company, a world leader in the manufacture of electrical controls, became interested in the city as a site for a new plant to manufacture circuit breakers. The Chamber of Commerce was again ready for this opportunity.

As part of its program to attract industries, the Chamber of Commerce had set up a civic planning committee, and this committee had an option on 54 acres of prime industrial land in the southwest section of the city. This land availability plus the other community and economic assets made the sale, and Square D's 120,000-square-foot plant was erected on the site. Designated as the circuit breaker division of Square D, this plant was put into operation in September 1955. Numerous additions and expansions more than doubled the plant's size.

In addition to its increased production capabilities, the local plant has become a center for national and international research and development for Square D.

Success followed success in the industrial development of this period. A year after the Square D plant was put into operation Cedar Rapids acquired a Downing Box Company plant. This Milwaukee-based firm was one of the leading manufacturers of corrugated paper boxes. The circumstances surrounding this new plant was an unusual chapter in the story of industrial development. Ordinarily, industrial development involves long and tedious months, sometimes years. Downing Box was the rare exception.

When the Square D plant was ready to be dedicated, the top executives of the company were invited in for a red-carpet dinner by the Chamber of Commerce. A key executive of Downing Box came along with the Square D group. Interested in seeing the plant, he was also interested in looking at Cedar Rapids. There had been no indication that Downing Box was looking for another plant location. Impressed with the city and its civic leaders, the Downing official made a fast decision. If a suitable site could be found, he would recommend that Cedar Rapids should have the new plant. A suitable site was found on Blairsferry Road N.E., and the plant opened in 1956.

Longview Fibre took over Downing Box in a merger in the late 1970s. It became known as the Central Container Division of Longview Fibre Company.

The next industrial addition to Cedar Rapids came in the early part of 1964. Armed with preliminary economic and demographic data on the city, an anon-

The Cedar Rapids plant of the Square D Company, located at 3700 Sixth St. S.W., houses the circuit breaker division and is an international research and development facility with an engineering staff and research laboratory. Photo by Thompson Photographers. Courtesy, Cedar Rapids Chamber of Commerce

ymous group of businessmen arrived in the city, contacted the Chamber of Commerce, and began discussion on the possibility of erecting a plant in the city. On February 21, 1964, the announcement was made that Miehle-Goss-Dexter, Inc., of Chicago would build a new plant in Cedar Rapids, a plant that would turn out the very latest in printing presses. Initial employment was projected at 400.

Several years before this, the Chamber of Commerce had the foresight to purchase the 138-acre Hunter Airport property for development as an industrial park. Fifty acres of this was now available for the plant. It was this immediate land availability, as well as the industrial image of Cedar Rapids, that prompted Miehle-Goss-Dexter to make their fast decision. It only took one trip to the land site for the company officials to visualize exactly how the plant would sit on the property. All that remained was for details to be worked out.

Ground was broken in July 1964, and the plant was dedicated on December 3, 1965. Production was started on web-offset presses for small weekly newspapers, but in June 1968 the plant was converted to the Metro-offset press designed for use by larger newspapers. Employment was substantially increased, and Cedar Rapids became a major center for the production of newspaper presses.

Late 1968 brought a flurry of corporate take-over offers for the parent company. North American Rockwell, Indian Head, Inc., Walter Kidde, Inc., and Continental Can all expressed deep interest in a possible merger and/or acquisition. North American Rockwell was successful, and by mid-1969 the merger was approved. The local plant name was changed to MGD Graphic Systems-North American Rockwell. By the end of the 1970s, the plant was turning out the Metroliner press, the largest unit in the company line.

Two other industries of the "Golden Thirty Years" era, both homegrown and launched in 1968, were organized by employee spinoffs from Collins Radio.

J-Tec, started in June 1968, was the brainchild of Theodore J. Johnson and Robert D. Joy. Johnson was a government contract specialist with Collins Radio, and Joy was a research engineer with the same firm. They formed the company to work in oceanographic and meteorological instrumentation, along with what they called "sociological electronics." The latter term was a coined one, relating electronics to urban growth.

In its early stages, J-Tec developed a flow meter that measured the flow force of wind or fluids. J-Tec also developed an underwater timer for use by the Navy in demolition. The company's track record throughout the years has resulted in several types of commercial-research projects, some of which have been with automobile or automobile-related industries.

In 1984 J-Tec received a contract for crosswind sensors that can be used on military tanks. This sensor determines "windage" to aid in accurately aiming the tank's guns. This has opened up a whole new field for the company, and augurs well for the future.

The second of these homegrown industries was started in mid-1968 by George Chadima, Robert Bruce, and Robert Steele. Chadima and Bruce were associated with Collins Radio. Steele left Remington Rand to join them in an effort to extend the computer revolution to small businesses. The result of their research was the Norand Corporation.

They established their first offices in the First Avenue Building where they spent about two years talking to small businesses to determine where the market was. They found that keeping track of inventory and the handling/ordering of merchandise was a major problem, particularly in the grocery or food business. They decided to work initially through wholesalers.

They sold their first order-entry system to Red Owl Food stores in 1970. Sales for that first year amounted to $400,000; five years later, their sales hit seven million dollars. Their operation was shifted to a new four-story headquarters office building at 550 Second Street S.E. They developed the portable electronic ordering system, and the portable shelf barcode scanner, both of which are extensively used to facilitate inventory control in grocery and other retail establishments.

With the purchase of the company by Pioneer Hi-Bred International of Des Moines in October 1976, Norand acquired additional financial structure. It has continued to expand its operations and its research development into various types of data and inventory-control systems. Its product lines are now in demand by soft-drink companies, fast-food chains, national food chains, purchasing associations, and food wholesalers.

The "Golden Thirty Years" was a unique period in the business/industrial development of Cedar Rapids. These years were unequalled in economic growth and vitality, in the successful promotion of the city to new business and industry, and in the marshaling of community resources.

Top: This circa 1910 image shows the first truck of the Cedar Rapids and Iowa City Railway & Electric Light Company, after the horse-and-wagon days. Courtesy, Iowa Electric Light & Power Company

Bottom left: This late nineteenth century arc light was used by the Baltimore Gas & Electric Company. This was the first stage of electrical lighting in the city. Courtesy, Iowa Electric Light & Power Company

Bottom right: These gas holding tanks of Iowa Illinois Gas held 500,000 cubic feet (in the right tank) and a million cubic feet (in the left tank). The larger tank was built in 1926, the smaller around 1903. This photograph was taken in 1951.

UTILITIES

The advent of utilities—gas, water, and electricity—has traditionally heralded the transition of a pioneer community into a modern community. It is also characteristic of utilities to start out as a service to the public, but as their scope expands and their technology advances, they become a business—a big business.

The gas industry arrived in Cedar Rapids in 1871. In the early days of the city, candles were the principal form of lighting. Whale oil was available, but was expensive—80 cents a gallon. The discovery of petroleum in Pennsylvania produced kerosene that cost much less, about 22 cents a gallon.

Business, however, looking for a better source of illumination, was interested in the coal-gas lighting in operation in the larger Eastern cities. In 1871 the first gas franchise in Cedar Rapids was issued to the W.H. Witta Company, which was authorized to operate a gas plant and lay mains in the city streets. The city then numbered about 6,000 residents.

Within the year this franchise was taken over by a new company, the Cedar Rapids Gaslight and Coke Company, organized by A.T. Averill, H.G. Higley, M.A. Higley, and John Thomas. They established their first modest gasworks at Seventh Avenue and First Street, and began to develop the city's gas mains system. By 1878 the company had laid eight miles of mains, had about 300 customers, and was servicing 115 street lamps.

At first the principal use of gas was for business and street illumination, but eventually the larger homes became users. Smaller homes still depended on kerosene lamps.

By the early 1880s, the city population was approaching the 15,000 mark. The gas company in 1884 constructed a new 100,000-cubic-foot gas holder and new buildings for auxiliary equipment. The new plant was located one block south of the old buildings, at Eighth Avenue and First Street. Residential use of gas continued to increase, and in 1887 a contract was secured to provide street illumination beyond the business district for the outlying areas of the city. The company employed a number of lamplighters who, at dusk, went from one streetlight to another, lighting each with a match. There were about five such routes in the city, with a total of about 300 lamps. Early in the morning, each lamp had to be turned off by hand.

Above: The general offices of Cedar Rapids Gas Company, set up in 1913 to take over the city's gas services, were at the corner of Third Street and Fourth Avenue S.E. Courtesy, Cedar Rapids Chamber of Commerce

Right: The Cedar Rapids Water Works went into operation in 1875 at D Avenue and Second Street N.E. It had five miles of water mains, primarily downtown, and was privately owned until 1903. The two-story building at right is the Cedar Rapids Boat Club, where the elite held dances and regattas. From Clements, Tales of the Town, 1967

Opposite: This 1899 picture shows an early electric generator, one of the first combined power and light units. It was designed by W.J. Greene, an early president of the Iowa Electric Light & Power Company. Courtesy, Iowa Electric Light & Power Company

Competition soon reared its head. Electricity—introduced in the city in 1882—had been constantly improved and refined for lighting purposes. In 1891 electric arc lights were installed in the business district. Eventually electricity won the bid for all the street illumination in Cedar Rapids.

Gas was able to retain business with the introduction of the Welsbach Gas Lamp which proved to be very popular not only in stores but also in homes. Gas appliances had become efficient and economical, and gas ranges had been successfully introduced in the early 1890s, requiring a 500,000-cubic-foot gas holder to be built in 1903. When Marion's gas plant was destroyed by an explosion in 1905, the Cedar Rapids company extended its mains to Marion.

In 1907 the city sought to put into effect a gas rate ordinance which the company fought bitterly. Litigation on the ordinance went on for three years. The

Cedar Rapids Gaslight and Coke Company eventually lost this costly litigation, and in the process exhausted its financial resources. In 1910 it came under the control of United Light and Power Company. In turn, the Cedar Rapids Gas Company was set up in 1913 to take over gas service in the city.

In 1926 Cedar Rapids became one of the first cities in the nation to have a one-million-cubic-foot gas holder. This waterless holder, the second of its type in the United States, was located at Ninth Avenue and First Street.

The early 1930s saw natural gas becoming a more economical substitute for coal gas, and by 1933 a pipeline was under construction from Ainsworth, Iowa, to Cedar Rapids. It reached Cedar Rapids on February 12, 1934, and natural gas began to flow through the 150 miles of pipelines in the Cedar Rapids area.

LOOMIS BROTHERS INC.

In May 1897 James C. and Charles C. Loomis formed a partnership—Loomis Brothers General Contractors and Builders. Today Loomis Brothers Inc. is the second-oldest such firm in the state.

Sons of Morgan Loomis, an Iowa pioneer, James and Charles attended Cedar Rapids schools, Cedar Rapids Business College, and Coe College. They mastered the carpenter's trade while employed by A.H. Connors, a local contractor. After forming their own business as general contractors in stone, brick, and wood, the brothers did considerable work in Cedar Rapids and the surrounding area. Their first construction project was the Home for the Friendless. Other major jobs included the Scottish Rite Temple, the Consistory, and the chapel, Science Hall, and Voorhees Hall at Coe College.

Charles E. Loomis, son of James, assumed control of the family business in the early 1930s. Buildings on which he worked included the Souvenir Lead Pencil Company, Pepsi-Cola Bottling Works, Link Belt Speeder, First Congregational Church, Wilson Company, Quaker Oats, Iowa Manufacturing Company, and several custombuilt homes.

His son, Charles E. Loomis, Jr., began working with the firm in 1946 after serving in the U.S. Army Corps of Engineers. He served as president of the company from 1961 to 1988, and is currently chairman of the board. David C. and James C., sons of Charles Loomis, Jr., comprise the fourth generation to be associated in the family business. David joined the firm in 1977 and currently serves as president. James joined the firm the following year and currently is vice-president.

Loomis Brothers is active in both general construction and

Above: Loomis Brothers Contractors, shown at the ground-breaking ceremony for the Coe College Science Building. Photo circa 1911

Top: The Loomis Brothers headquarters is located at 1619 F Avenue Northeast in Cedar Rapids and is operated by the Loomis family. As a general contractor and builder, the firm employs approximately 100 people.

construction management. Major construction projects in recent years include United Fire and Casualty Company, KCRG Studios, the Coe College Fine Arts Building, Cornell College Life Sports Center, Teleconnect corporate office building, St. Luke's Ambulatory Surgery Center, Grinnell College Library additions, Pfaff Building renovation, Higley/Law Complex, and Downtown Skyway System.

Current projects include St. Luke's Hospital, Coe College Library, Luther College-Koren renovation, Holiday Inn-Iowa City, and Armstrong's Department Store renovation.

Loomis Brothers Inc. is affiliated with Associated General Contractors of America and is a charter member of Master Builders of Iowa.

ROCKWELL INTERNATIONAL

Rockwell International Corporation is Cedar Rapids' largest company, employing some 8,700 people and occupying 2.5 million square feet of manufacturing and office space. Rockwell entered the Cedar Rapids business community through the acquisition of two prominent local enterprises.

In 1969 Rockwell purchased Miehle-Goss-Dexter Company, which had operated in the community for four years. This firm, which commands a major share of the market in large printing presses, now operates as Graphics Systems Division.

Rockwell's largest Cedar Rapids acquisition came in 1973, when it purchased Collins Radio Company. Founded in 1931 by Arthur Collins, this local business flourished on the strength of its founder's technological creativity. Collins equipment attained a worldwide reputation for innovation and quality. Under Rockwell, the former Collins Radio Company in Cedar Rapids has been divided into two major business units. The Avionics Group manufactures aviation electronics (known in the industry as avionics). Collins Defense Communications (CDC) specializes in communication equipment. Cedar Rapids serves as the headquarters for both the Avionics Group and CDC as they manage operations throughout the United States and Canada.

While the products of Rockwell's Avionics Group bear little resemblance to those on which Arthur Collins founded Collins Radio Company, the desire for quality and innovation continues to drive the firm toward international acceptance. This fact is borne out by the reputation Collins-brand equipment holds in world markets. Through the Avionics Group's three divisions—Collins Air Transport, Collins General Aviation, and Collins Government Avionics—the group designs, develops, manufactures, and services communication,

navigation, and flight-control products for a wide array of national and international customers. These include some of the leading airplane manufacturers: Boeing, McDonnell Douglas, Fokker, Lockheed, and Airbus Industrie. Beech Aircraft Corporation, Cessna, Dassault-Breguet, British Aerospace, and others also rely on Collins avionics equipment, as do the U.S. armed forces and governments worldwide.

In addition, the firm works on the frontiers of technology with the likes of the Navstar Global

Above: The Advanced Railroad Electronics System developed by Avionics Group will use Global Positioning System positioning capability and technologies for communication, control, and display to modernize the railroad industry.

Left: The "C" Avenue Northeast complex of Rockwell International, located between Collins Road and Blairs Ferry Road. Headquarters of CDC are at the lower right; Avionics Group facilities are across "C" Avenue in the center of the photo.

The Graphic Systems Division's two-building facililty in Cedar Rapids manufactures Goss Colorliner and Flexoliner printing presses for the newspaper industry.

New Goss printing presses are staged at the Graphic Systems Division's Cedar Rapids facility.

Positioning System. This system uses orbiting satellites to provide precise, three-dimensional navigation information for land, sea, and air operations anywhere in the world.

The group's advanced technology scientists are at work researching methods of producing miniaturized electronics products that can replace large printed circuit boards with tiny, multichip modules and flat-panel video displays to replace today's deep picture tubes.

Copper coils and vacuum tubes, the early components of the first radios, have become part of the rich legacy of the Collins Radio Company handed down to Collins Defense Communications.

CDC occupies the former Collins engineering building on "C" Avenue and the historic main plant facility on 35th Street. But today solid-state electronics have replaced wires and coils; leadless components on interchangeable circuit cards have replaced vacuum tubes; and fiber-optic cables have brought advanced communications to the world at the speed of light.

CDC is a major supplier of advanced communication products, systems, and service to the U.S. Department of Defense, NATO allies, and more than 40 countries worldwide. Products and systems virtually cover the frequency spectrum and are utilized in every aspect of the U.S. Minimum Essential Emergency Communications Network (MEECN). Radios small enough to carry are employed by ground troops while other communications systems fill 747 jet aircraft to provide vital communications links from U.S. Command Authorities to armed forces deployed worldwide.

CDC is also producing satellite terminals to meet tri-service communications requirements that reach into the twenty-first century. On the ground, in Cedar Rapids,

An operator at Collins Defense Communications' high-technology manufacturing facility sets up the computerized "Pick and Place" machine used to place electronic components on circuit boards. The robot can select, test, and place as many as 2,000 components an hour.

CDC's Communications Central continues its long tradition of 24-hour-a-day, seven-day-a-week radio communications for federal agencies and ships at sea.

Rockwell International's Graphic Systems Division is the world's leading supplier of newspaper production systems. The division is also a major manufacturer of commercial offset printing presses, and markets sheet-fed presses and bindery equipment.

The division's Goss presses are recognized as the standard in the newspaper industry. Goss presses print two out of three U.S. daily newspapers and some of the most prestigious newspapers in 95 countries.

The Cedar Rapids plant was established in 1965. It was more than doubled in size through the purchase of an adjacent building and property in 1987. The two-building facility uses the latest computer-aided manufacturing technology to produce state-of-the-art products.

The expansion of manufacturing facilities reflects the sales success of presses such as the new Goss Colorliner—a press that has met the newspaper industry's demand for improved print quality with expanded page capacity and color capability. As newspapers install these sophisticated new presses, readers and advertisers can expect high-quality color printing on many more pages of their daily paper.

THE GAZETTE

When the *Cedar Rapids Daily Gazette* began publication on January 10, 1883, Cedar Rapids had already experienced more than 30 years of newspaper publication. Its first weekly, *The Progressive Era*, had started in 1851, followed by a series of weekly publications under various names and ownerships. The concept of a daily paper had been started in 1870 by the *Cedar Rapids Republican*.

At the time *The Gazette* began publishing, there were four other newspapers already in operation in the city, and competition was keen. The first issue of *The Gazette* was four small pages, and it contained exactly 70 words of telegraph news, three columns of local news, a few filler features, plus a few indifferent advertisements. Reception by the existing papers and the advertisers in general was somewhat less than positive. It was not an auspicious beginning.

A year later the paper was about to go out of business. One of the co-publishers had already severed his connections and had left town, and the remaining co-publisher was so discouraged that he was ready to fold the paper. Circulation was only 1,500 copies and wavering. Then two local men,

Clarence L. Miller and Fred W. Faulkes, took over the company, and under their business and editorial policies, the paper began to grow. They changed it to an eight-column publication and pushed the circulation to 2,000. As Cedar Rapids and eastern Iowa grew, *The Gazette* grew in circulation and advertising.

With success and expansion came the need for larger facilities. The first home of *The Gazette* was at what is now 309 First Avenue Southeast in the Hazeltine building. The paper made another move in 1885, then three years later acquired a new location on the corner of First Avenue and First Street, where the Federal Building now sits. This new home was the most modern newspaper plant in the state, and it served the paper for

36 years. In 1925 *The Gazette* moved to its present location.

The Gazette continues to grow, both in size and in newspaper technology. Today the newspaper operation is highly computerized, utilizing the very latest in offset presses and a newly acquired digital color scanner. Its facilities are state of the art. This progressive technological philosophy has won many awards for *The Gazette* in writing, photography, design, color usage, technical excellence, and community service, including the coveted Pulitzer Prize.

Its active leadership role in community affairs, its sponsorship of numerous special events each year, and its Newspaper in Education program distinguish *The Cedar Rapids Gazette* as a good community citizen.

Above: Today the latest in newspaper technology is applied, including offset presses and a digital color scanner.

At left: The Gazette occupied this location on First Avenue, which was considered the most modern newspaper plant in the state, from 1888 to 1924.